Sunshine and Ice
Volume 10

Glittering Stars

MARTIN MONEY

Published by New Generation Publishing in 2016

Copyright © Martin Money 2016

First Edition

ISBN: 978-1-78507-856-9

www.newgeneration-publishing.com

New Generation Publishing

GLITTERING STARS

Part One

December 2014 to March 2015

INTRODUCTION – FLEXIBLE WORDS

Tolerance is a funny word, isn't it? – One of dozens with a glaringly obvious meaning hiding an intriguing paradox. It's deceptively flexible when it comes to its application.

Readers of my previous books will know that I'm a firm advocate of tolerance as most widely understood – that is, indicating a display of acceptance and respect for worldviews and lifestyles that challenge your own.

It's a basic human right to believe what you want and live your life the way you wish. Our world would be a much nicer place if everyone showed a lot more tolerance towards others' religious, political, sexual and social attitudes and behaviour.

With one crucial condition, of course – that those views and actions don't threaten or impinge upon anyone else's wellbeing or their similar rights to hold opinions and express them in a peaceful, non-violent way.

For that's when the word tolerance takes on a totally different meaning. I avidly support freedom of speech, but I won't tolerate it when hate-fuelled words incite harmful actions or the brutal enforcement of oppressive policies.

Oh look, there's another flexible word – hate. So is love for that matter. For example, I try to spread the love, combat hatred and do whatever I can to strengthen the healing positive vibration and weaken the destructive negative one.

But I still hate the way some people appear to love inflicting pain and misery on others. See what I mean?

Such is the strange fascination of the English language. But I still revel in using and playing with its words. It's a wonderful way to communicate a range of human feelings and experiences.

Which is what I do with my writing – the prose and verse I put in my books.

So here we go again. *Sunshine and Ice Volume Ten*, as yet untitled.

I shall continue to try and entertain with my unique and arguably strange take on our crazy existence. I also hope to foster the positive while helping oust the negative.

If my oddball observations, loopy lyrics and deranged declarations inspire just one person to promote the good vibe a bit more and help enrich the lives of others, I'll consider that success indeed. More people would be better.

Anyway, without further ado, here's the latest instalment…

****

CHAPTER ONE – A SHARP JOLT

December 16 – Oh dear oh dear! We've been brought back to Earth with a sharp jolt. The festive feel good factor has been viciously shunted aside by two shocking events.

At least 120 people, most of them children, have been killed in a Taliban assault on an army-run school in Peshawar, Pakistan, according to official sources.

Meanwhile, in Australia, we're told that a gunman and two of his hostages died as commandos stormed a café in Sydney in order to bring to an end a 16-hour siege.

The gunman, named as Man Haron Monis, was said to have forced some of his prisoners to hold up a black Islamic banner at the window of the café.

So, it seems, Muslim fundamentalists have been making their presence felt again. Or is it a case of opportunistic psychos cynically using growing ideological tension as an excuse to unleash their own unhinged ultra-violent tendencies?

Who knows? Well one thing's for sure, anyone in power who knows the truth won't be sharing it with us any time soon.

As an eternal optimist, I was kinda hoping that 2015 would prove a pivotal year in history – one in which religious and cultural differences were finally recognized and respected and we moved forward at last towards a more peaceful future.

The chances of that happening are seemingly receding by the day. But I continue to dream, convinced that throwing in the towel and accepting the bloodstained status quo as inevitable really would be a criminal desertion of our shared responsibility.

It also worries me deeply when so-called Islamic extremists are the only ones singled out. Their actions sicken and abhor me but armed nut-jobs citing religion and politics in attempts justify murder and mayhem can be found across the ideological spectrum.

And yet we don't hear much about – for example – Israeli loonies claiming they're devout Jews while kicking the crap out of Palestinian Muslims in the Gaza Strip, or those purporting to be Christians inflicting pain and death on a global scale.

We quite rightly get all steamed up when crazies professing to be Islamists behead our soldiers and aid workers. But we turn a blind eye to the same shocking and grisly practice in Saudi Arabia, where it's employed by the state as the ultimate punishment.

Of course, it's not up to us how other countries enforce their laws – just like it's not up to them how we run our justice system. But we can make our disapproval known.

I'm just pinpointing the infuriating inconsistency and blatant hypocrisy being shown in certain quarters.

Oh, silly me! – Just remembered, Israel and Saudi Arabia are our rich and generous friends and allies. People there can apparently do no wrong – at least until these nations fall out of favour. And that's not very likely at present, is it?

Let's be crystal clear here. I'll re-iterate what I've said many times – I have absolutely nothing against any race of people or their chosen faiths or ideologies, just so long as they don't use hate-laced rhetoric, brutal control, icy elitism or deadly discrimination.

My beef is with the homicidal maniacs who hijack then twist spiritual or political beliefs in order to enforce them in a violent and divisive way.

And they can be found everywhere. Yes, even here, in England. In our communities and the corridors of power. Terrifying I know but tragically true.

My attitude to all these murderous meatheads is you're certainly no proper Christian, Jew, Muslim or whatever. You represent an odious insult to the faith you profess yet cruelly pervert. And your insane claim to be in any way religious turns my stomach.

You should ruddy well crawl back under whichever stone you slid out from beneath and leave the rest of us in peace.

But enough of serious and unnerving heavy stuff. Methinks it's time to let the Christmas spirit dominate our thoughts again.

December 18 – Back in a celebratory groove, I'd like to wish a very happy ninth birthday to Leon, my great mate Kerry's son, and also extend birthday greetings to Sue Bolton, a former work colleague and drinking buddy.

Sue put a photo of me on Facebook yesterday, taken at one of our Krypton/Mace works Christmas meals. And she was on TV last night – in a group of people used for the video of Sir Cliff Richard's festive number one hit song Saviour's Day.

December 21 – Yuletide salutations to one and all. Yep, it's the winter solstice again – the shortest day of the year, sacred to pagans and followers of the nature religions.

December 24 – Happy birthday to my dear friend Carole Jones. Have a blinder, love.

While I'm trying to keep this upbeat for the festive season, the big bad world continues to invade all our thoughts – as usual!

Glasgow residents are in shocked mourning after a bin lorry crashed in a busy street, killing six people and injuring 10.

Christmas lights across Scotland have been turned off as a mark of respect for the victims.

Gravel-voiced rock star Joe Cocker has died aged 70 after battling against lung cancer.

Sheffield-born Cocker is probably best known for his soulful rendering of the Beatles' song With a Little Help from My Friends – and Sir Paul McCartney has led the tributes, saying he was a "good mate and a lovely guy."

Elsewhere in the world, it's the usual fare of murders, disease, unrest and misery. Bad news has no respect for Christmas, it seems.

December 25 – Well, it's the big day itself. Earlier today I put festive greetings on Facebook, took a phone call from my son Phil, opened my presents, sent a text to my sister Carol and phoned my Auntie Joyce.

My festive gifts included W H Smiths tokens, cookies, chocolates, money and a soup bowl, plate and spoon set.

I'm having a quiet and chilled day but later I'm off to Sam and Carl's for a buffet meal and drinkies. Cool!

December 27 – It's Saturday today and I've had a jolly good Crimbo. The festive buffet was great and we had several weird cocktails with our usual chosen tipples, in my case cans of lager. Jem joined us and a good time was had by all.

Among my presents from Sam and family was a "onesie" – the first I've possessed. It'll come in handy with the weather getting decidedly colder.

Sam, bless her, invited me back yesterday – Boxing Day – for lunch and more drinkies. But she, Carl and I were all pretty wiped out after the previous day's craziness so I left early evening. It was a great couple of days, though – cheers guys!

Come to think of it, I had a few pints in the Bell on Christmas Eve too, so no wonder I was feeling like I'd had enough by yesterday tea-time!

Today's going to be a no-alcohol day. In fact I'm knocking the booze on the head until Wednesday, New Year's Eve.

After that, it'll be back to my normal low-fat, limited alcohol regime, which largely goes out of the window over the festive period as I quaff more drink than usual and scoff pork pies, chocolate, snacks and other high-fat foods.

But that's the point I guess – being quite strict with myself for the rest of the time means I can push the boat out a bit on special occasions without doing too much damage.

And the less you have of anything nice, the more you enjoy it when you do. And I do like pork pies!

So, all in all, I've had another good Christmas. I really love this time of year, even though for me, like many people, the jolly vibes are tinged with sadness, a mourning and longing for those no longer with us in this physical plane but always in our hearts.

People such as my dear old Dad, who would have been celebrating his 99th birthday today had he not passed over aged 68. RIP guiding light – I've got a candle burning for you and I've put a little tribute on Facebook, you wise, kind funny man.

It's also the birthday of Martine, Jem's daughter. I've sent her a Facebook message.

December 28 – And another birthday – this time of my mate Scott Collins, Kerry's partner. Scott loves football, studies the sports pages of the daily papers and is really well informed. He knows more about Man U than I do – and he's an Arsenal fan!

But back to that tinge of sadness. Tom text me the other day to say he'd heard that two old friends of ours, Sue and Steve Meadowcroft, had both died recently.

Such a shame. They were younger than me. The couple were members of the old 1970s/80s rock'n'roll revival crowd we knocked about with in those golden Pinecliff/ Palmerston/White Horse,/Hop Inn/Home Guard days.

Ah, sweet memories! RIP guys.

December 30 – 2.30 pm – I've just had a wonderful festive visit from Phil, Emily and Chloe. They popped over to give me my Christmas present, a really cool "legends" double CD set featuring pop and rock's biggest stars, and spend a bit of time with me.

Chloe's a little pickle who I've nicknamed "Hurricane" thanks to the whirlwind effect she had on my flat. I adore her. Neither Lucas nor Harvey, my equally adorable grandsons, could make it this time. But it was still a Christmas highlight. Fantastic!

January 1, 2015 – Happy New Year everybody! Let's hope 2015 is going to be a good one all round.

Or at least as far as possible. Sadly, there are always those facing crisis and pain – like Pauline Cafferkey, the first Brit to be diagnosed with the dreaded Ebola virus.

Ms Cafferkey, an associate public health nurse who normally works at the Blantyre Health Centre in South Lanarkshire, had been working in the dangerous "red zone" near Freetown in Sierra Leone.

She was diagnosed with the lethal disease after returning to Scotland from Sierra Leone via Casablanca and London Heathrow.

She was later transferred to a specialist treatment centre at the Royal Free Hospital in London, where she's in strict isolation and her condition is said to be stable.

Oh dear – so the highly infectious killer virus with no known cure has now reached our shores. Is this the great end-of-the-world plague as predicted in the Book of Revelations? Probably not – but it's still a very worrying state of affairs.

This fresh spate of Ebola has so far claimed more than 8,000 lives. As the fight against the deadly epidemic continues, scientists believe they might have pinpointed where the outbreak started.

They think a two-year-old boy in the West African country of Guinea could have contracted the virus as he played in a hollowed out tree used by a colony of fruit bats.

Also on the news, a New Year stampede in China has killed 35 people and wounded 42 others.

The crush happened just before midnight in the historic Bund riverside district in Shanghai, where thousands of people had gathered to see in 2015.

So the world continues to spin on its axis and people continue to suffer and die. But I still hope that as many as possible enjoy a pleasant and satisfying year.

January 3 – As if to ram home the bad news point in that last paragraph, we now hear of two more upsetting tragedies.

An AirAsia plane crashed into the sea with 162 people on board while flying from Indonesia to Singapore. No survivors have been found and the cause of its plummet remains unknown.

So far, 30 bodies have been recovered as crash investigators continue to work at the site, in the Java Sea.

Meanwhile, fears are growing for the fates of 98 passengers still unaccounted for after a car ferry caught fire in the Adriatic. The search for bodies has been severely hampered by storms.

The Norman Atlantic vessel sailed from Greece on Sunday, reportedly with 478 people on board.

January 7 – Ye gods! Yet more bad news, this time involving an apparent terrorist attack in France.

Gunmen stormed the Paris office of the satirical magazine, *Charlie Hebdo*, killing 12 people and injuring seven.

Two police officers were said to be among the fatalities in the atrocity, quickly condemned by French President Francois Hollande, German Chancellor Angela Merkel, David Cameron, Barack Obama and other world leaders.

No-one has yet claimed responsibility.

January 8 – And another fatal gun incident in Paris! Gordon bleedin' Bennett!

A female cop has reportedly died of her injuries after she and a colleague were shot in the city's southern sector this morning.

It comes within 24 hours of the *Charlie Hebdo* massacre. Authorities believe it's just shocking, grisly coincidence and the two incidents aren't linked, but it's still a terrible double whammy for France and the wider world that looks on aghast.

Two men with assault rifles are said to have shot at the officers after their car was involved in a road accident. One gunman was apparently arrested. The other fled.

Meanwhile, a major police operation is underway to find three gunmen who fled by car after yesterday's gun attack on the magazine.

Witnesses have apparently reported hearing the gunmen shouting "We have avenged the Prophet Muhammad" and "Allahu Akbar" ("God is Great" in Arabic).

Here we go again – yet another strong suggestion that Islamic extremists have launched a terrorist attack on innocent people.

Whoever's responsible, they're clearly bloodlust crazies with no sense of humour. The dead weren't violent militant warmongers; they were editorial staff – satirists boldly upholding freedom of speech and expression.

Sure, they pulled no punches in lampooning religious and political absurdities. But good on 'em I say.

I suppose the equivalent here would be a killing spree at the *Private Eye* office, an axe assault on the Monty Python team or bumping off the creators of Spitting Image.

Or in the US, the assassination of Seth MacFarlane, the irreverent boundary-ignoring wag behind the satirical cartoon shows Family Guy and American Dad.

People often glibly declare that the pen is mightier than the sword. Well, I for one am not that eager to test the theory in open combat. But there's a core principle at stake here.

It's called freedom. And it's under threat. I find that despicable and alarming.

Another word for freedom is liberty, one of the three ideals of the French Revolution that overthrew its monarchy in favour of the republic we still see today.

So the bloodstained attack on the *Charlie Hebdo* staff strikes at the very heart of that nation's vision and identity.

I'm both moved and encouraged by the response to the atrocity. The French don't tolerate unfair, unjust and oppressive behaviour like others, including us, can at times.

They, and the wider world community, are basically saying "stuff you violent killers – we will not be silenced and you'll never defeat us, because we believe in democracy and freedom of expression."

I'm not talking about the politicians here – they can sod off too, because their insane and unjust policies are largely responsible for the unfairness, splits and resentment that spark violence and war.

No, I'm referring to the amazing, wonderful, glorious, unbreakable human spirit that refuses to yield to the terrorizing presence and lethal actions of oppressive bullies.

Keep the faith, shine those lights and never stop chasing off the dark, brutal, negative forces that try to run our reality. And please don't lose your sense of humour!

I'm listening to The Very Best of The Proclaimers as I type this. The Scottish duo, comprising identical twin brothers Craig and Charlie Reid, really impress with their soft rock songs tinged by folk and country. Their music is good, their lyrics great.

January 9 – Vicious thugs, sick perverts, selfish gits, bullies, lazy liabilities, robbers, liars, cheats, adulterers, cowards… I could go on with the list of deeply insulting labels people chuck around so liberally and carelessly.

All are highly judgemental, vivid and emotive descriptions and they encompass a wide range of human frailties.

But when you think about it, who hasn't been guilty of at least one of the activities – serious or otherwise – indicated by these graphic terms at one time or another in their lives?

I'll give you two examples – those loaded words cheat and liar. Both pointedly signify bad behaviour.

If a worker fiddles their expenses, they're cheating the firm out of money. On the face of it, that's clearly wrong. But what if their boss pays the legal minimum while constantly berating them, demanding they go the extra mile without a trace of thanks?

And what about the little white fibs that help prevent friction and keep the peace or avoid hurting someone's feelings, even making them feel better?

To turn the argument on its head, pride is often considered a virtue, as in "I'm too proud to accept charity."

As someone who has on occasions been too damned poor to be proud, I see this attitude as self-defeating folly displaying arrogance, a stubborn refusal to face hard facts and a nasty, ungrateful snub of an offer of help or another's generous nature.

Speaking of pride, may I also remind its slavish servants that it's actually one of the seven deadly sins as cited in Christianity?

The others, of course, are lust, gluttony, greed, sloth, wrath and envy.

Then there are the 10 Commandments – to serve God, not make graven images or blaspheme, to observe the Sabbath day, honour your parents, never kill, commit adultery or steal, and not to bear false witness or covet anything your peers have.

Crikey – put all that lot together and we're in the realms of fantasy. Someone who's never done or said something covered by any of the above just ain't flipping human!

But when it comes to poor behaviour, we can all be very selective in our judgement – condoning certain bad traits while flying into a wild rage at others.

A guy handy with his fists or a baseball bat might beat up someone whose actions have affected him or his loved ones, totally ignoring the golden rule that two wrongs don't make a right.

Yet we might have a certain degree of sympathy with a person who lies and deceives to benefit or protect others, steals to feed their families or finds comfort in the arms of someone else after many miserable years locked in a loveless marriage to a selfish, abusive partner.

Having said that, I do believe that sexual cheating is, generally speaking, a definite no-no and people should have the guts and decency to finish one relationship before starting another.

At the end of the day, all the above actions are wrong – no question – even though they may be justified, even acceptable in certain circumstances.

Good people often feel forced to bend the rules for various reasons. On the other hand, some manage to be just plain obnoxious without doing much wrong.

One key factor here is who benefits – a self-centred, greedy, horrible person would only be interested in assisting themselves, a nicer individual might be driven by the desire to help others in need.

But hypocrites in deluded denial of their own faults are much too fast in being overly judgemental of others. It really makes me seethe.

We all have dark sides, you know!

Oh, and getting back briefly to what I was saying yesterday about freedom of speech and expression, this does mean accepting someone else's right to say something you might find obnoxious or even deeply insulting.

This can apply equally to hate-fuelled rhetoric or a satirical comment or cartoon.

Grown-up, balanced people can take all this on the chin. Only the infantile and violently unhinged use such modes of expression as excuses for bloodlust carnage.

Meanwhile, shocked millions of all faiths and none are repelled and appalled.

January 10 – French security forces yesterday killed two brothers suspected of taking part in the *Charlie Hebdo* attack after raiding a printing facility where they had holed up with a hostage. The hostage was freed unharmed, it's said.

Meanwhile, at a separate siege in a Paris kosher supermarket, four people and a gunman holding them were killed, according to NBC News. Police are searching for a woman said to be an accomplice of the suspected hostage-taker.

It is thought the two incidents might well be linked. Fanatical Muslims are being held responsible while it appears Jews were under attack in the shop siege.

So growing ethnic tension has sparked stunning lethal violence in our European neighbour country. It's also on the rise here. So is right-wing intolerance. Oh dear!

Meanwhile, 2,000 people are feared dead after a massacre in Nigeria, said to be the work of militant Islamic group Boko Haram.

It's truly shocking but before we pin all the blame for the world's troubles on Muslim extremists, let's please remember that homicidal crazies can profess a variety of beliefs and they come in all shapes, colours and sizes.

So do dozy pillocks for that matter. And that's my thought for today.

January 11, 5pm – I've just got back from a great day out in Poole for Harvey's fourth birthday.

Phil and Emily held a party for him at Pirates and Princesses, a super soft play facility and family café in the town's Dolphin shopping centre.

The whole gang attended – Harvey, Lucas, Chloe, Em's parents, her brother Simon, her sister Rachel and baby Lily, Joe, Cheryl, her daughter Kayleigh and son Ben, Phil's stepsister Ali, her partner Terry, their little girl Roxanna and other relatives and friends.

It was great to see everyone again and a special thrill when all three of my grandchildren made a fuss of me. Chloe and Harvey got me to dance with them – well sort of – in the disco room and Lucas sat on my lap more than once.

I also got to hold Lily for the first time.

Occasions like that are priceless and I was delighted to have the opportunity to go along.

January 12 – While we were celebrating Harvey's birthday, over the Channel in France 3.7 million people took to the streets in protest at the *Charlie Hebdo* killings.

Citizens of all faiths – including Muslims – took part in the massive show of solidarity for the core principle of freedom in the face of terrorist attacks.

This side of the pond, Tower Bridge and Trafalgar Square were among London landmarks lit up in red, white and blue, the shared colours of the French and British flags, in single-minded support.

It was a massive and powerful display of defiance, sending out a clear message that we stand together and will never tolerate murderous acts of violence. I applaud it.

The only sour note was the politicians who muscled in and tried to hijack the event – a stomach-turning sight as their unfair, unjust actions at home and abroad tend to aggravate the cultural splits that lead to tension and bloody conflict.

While French and British authorities stay on high alert, David Cameron was said to be meeting security and intelligence chiefs here today to discuss what extra measures might be needed to combat terror threats in our fair land.

I'd suggest an urgent review of aggressive foreign policies might be a start.

****

CHAPTER TWO – CREATURE COMFORTS

January 20 – There was a documentary on telly last night that I found interesting and disturbing in equal measure.

Called 'Angry, White and Proud', it was about the rise of the militant far-right groups that take to our streets to fight both Muslims and the police who get in their way.

To call it shocking would be a massive understatement. The ugly attitudes and behaviour on display were chilling and sickening.

And this came from the hard-line Islamists featured as much as their bigoted rivals.

But from what I saw, first blood in the violent clashes was actually being drawn by over-zealous coppers fanning the flames rather than keeping the peace.

It's a tinderbox scenario for sure that elected politicians should address and try to defuse as a matter of urgency before it escalates into a full-blown sectarian war.

This is serious stuff, deadly serious – a very real and growing threat to the democracy most of us purport to believe in.

And yet MPs seem more interested in chucking insults at the combatants than doing anything constructive to locate and deal with the causes of the bitter unrest.

In fact, their own biased and divisive actions, inflammatory language and total failure to grasp the nettle of disastrous immigration policies have all aggravated the situation.

Channel Four has never shied away from controversy and this alarming hour-long programme was no exception.

I just hope the politicians fishing for votes in May's general election take note and put this issue at the top of their agendas – but with sensitivity and efficiency, not just provocatively slating extremists from either side.

As for the Muslim-hating hard nuts featured, they seemed to be run-of-the-mill, ordinary, otherwise decent blokes enraged by government inefficiency and failure.

I despise their aggressive words and actions – but I do understand their frustration with our political masters who have shown themselves to be stunningly brutal in many respects but totally ineffectual in dealing with issues that really matter.

Having said that, I still think it's high time we as a nation – regardless of our religious beliefs – seized back our English flag and dear old Saint George from the extremists who have stolen them and turned them into emblems of bigotry and violence.

Angry, White and Proud was bold, thought-provoking and unsettling – riveting television for all the wrong reasons.

And talking of TV, another small screen icon has gone. Anne Kirkbride, who played Deirdre Barlow in Coronation Street for 42 years, passed away yesterday in a Manchester hospital after a short illness.

She was only 60 but had battled both cancer and depression. She will be greatly missed by the Corrie cast and crew and a nation that took her to its collective heart.

January 21 – Those who have read my inane ramblings thus far will have gathered that I love watching the soaps and a variety of other TV programmes just as much as I love listening to my CDs.

Between them, they give me access to hours of entertainment provided by a mesmerising array of glittering stars in the fields of music, comedy and drama.

Telly also provides an insight into the more serious side of life through its news channels and documentaries such as Angry, White and Proud.

Those pesky adverts aside, it's the source of much joy and information. It also provides inspiration for my lyrics.

A new one started forming in my mind as I watched the Jeremy Kyle Show yesterday. It went like this:

No Woman I Know

Martin Money, January 20, 2015

The lie detector proves that he's a dirty cheating rat
As TV viewers curse the git for treating her like that
They wonder why she stays with him and puts herself through hell
But love is blind and she's too kind as this guy knows so well

He says he's sorry, that he'll change, he promises the moon
But everyone is quite convinced he'll stray again real soon
Well, everyone but her that is – she's stubborn in denial
She won't take heed and break away from treatment oh so vile

He wins her back with soft words and a kiss
No woman that I know would put up with this

He breaks her heart and makes her cry, he disrespects her bad
She takes it all and won't walk out although he makes her sad
And then he dries her tears once more with flowers and a plan
Can tigers change their stripes? – No way! – But this girl thinks
    they can

He wins her back with soft words and a kiss
No woman that I know would put up with this.

January 22 – Television and my music system – Oh yes, they're among my most cherished creature comforts. But it's my family and friends who supply the love and companionship.

Speaking of which, happy birthday John… my pal John Gaynor that is, the Arsenal and Bournemouth fan who's been a drinking buddy of mine at the Bell for quite a few years now. Have a good one, mate.

After inputting the lyrics to No Woman I Know, I had further thoughts about how deceit and disrespect could be taken into darker territory, as happens with some couples when one is allowed to get away with bad behaviour so pushes it further.

Not content with constantly hurting their partner's feelings, they turn violent as well as horrid, posing an increasing threat to their victim's mental and physical welfare.

This is more likely to be the man viciously manipulating the woman. But it could be the other way round and also happens in same-sex relationships.

So the existing verses and chorus could run into the second song lyric like so:

THE NEXT LEVEL

Martin Money, January 21–22, 2015

...He's taking it to the next level, taking it to the next level,
Taking it to the next level now

There's violence creeping in here as he tightens his control
He starts to use his fists as she becomes his old rag doll
Her spirit's truly broken and she's lost all trace of will
She's pregnant with his baby and he says he loves her still

The ring upon her finger makes her think there's always hope
She's shut out all her loved ones and her mind is messed by dope
He's got her where he wants her while he cheats and cheats again
Then pampers her like crazy, buying presents – now and then

She's frightened and confused
She knows she's being abused
But loves him, praying that he changes soon

He pushes and he punches and he gives her quite a slap
Her self-esteem's rock bottom and that's why she takes the crap
She's feeling like a caged bird and she doesn't often smile

But fleeting pleasant moments make her think it's all worthwhile

Bruises hidden by her wedding dress
A woman with child don't need this stress

She's frightened and confused
She knows she's being abused
But loves him, praying that he changes soon – not a chance!

January 22 – several hours later – And here's a brand new lyric inspired by the Kyle show in general:

HATE PARADE

Martin Money, January 22, 2015

A nasty procession of hate and abuse
Unleashed through our telly sets
The people are dolts, the programme's a farce
And this is as mad as it gets

The hard-hearted host so likes winding them up
Till anger is all that we see
With heavies on hand to keep them at bay
He goads and insults them with glee

His vicious agenda's old fashioned and wrong
His ego's as big as the sun
His audience loves him – I can't fathom why
To them he's their own chosen one

It's a sign of our times –
Our unsettled age
Of splits and resentment
Suspicion and rage
I feel it's high time
We turned a new page
I'm hoping that people agree

This show's a disgrace with its morons as guests –
The cold dregs of humanity
So why do we watch it and like it so much?
Why is it compelling TV?

It's a sign of our times –
Our unsettled age
Of splits and resentment
Suspicion and rage
I feel it's high time
We turned a new page
I'm hoping that people agree

A nasty procession of hate and abuse
Unleashed through our telly sets
The people are dolts, the programme's a farce
And this is as mad as it gets

It's a sign of our times –
Our unsettled age
Of splits and resentment
Suspicion and rage
I feel it's high time
We turned a new page
I'm hoping that people agree.

January 23 – And here's a set of words written today, based on the TV documentary Angry, White and Proud:

FIRE AND BLOOD

Martin Money, January 23, 2015

There was a time blacks, gays and Jews were in the bigots' sights
But things have changed, it's others now they target in their fights

Fists of fury, fire and blood
Crush those Muslims in the mud
Kick 'em with your booted feet
Leave 'em lying in the street

Saint George tattoos, England flags
Foreigners are dirty slags
Take our land back, chuck 'em out
Leave the buggers in no doubt – we ain't messing!

United force, armed of course, and we ain't messing – oh no, we
ain't messing

Swords of vengeance, words of hate
Fighting for Islamic State
Make 'em suffer, give 'em hell
Smash the evil infidel

Fists of fury, fire and blood
Crush tormentors in the mud
Kick 'em with your booted feet
Leave 'em lying in the street

There was a time peace, love and hope were buzzwords used a lot
I still believe in those ideals but look at what we've got

Saint George tattoos, England flags
Foreigners are dirty slags
Take our land back, chuck 'em out
Leave the buggers in no doubt – we ain't messing!

United force, armed of course, and we ain't messing – oh no, we
*   ain't messing*
Leave the buggers in no doubt – we ain't messing!

Oh, and while we're on the subject of song words, here's a little
snippet that also came to me this week – a bit of a homage to the
rock music I love:

With lyrics so colourful, music so sweet
Those rock and roll poets make my life complete.

(Martin Money, January 20, 2015)

That's all I've got so far. Will inspiration strike again soon? Who
knows? I'll keep you posted.

January 25 – Once again I feel the need to explain myself.

Reading back the words to Hate Parade, it suddenly occurred to me
that my reference to "the cold dregs of humanity" could be
construed as a snobbish put-down of the so-called lower classes.

This was not my intention at all. I was alluding to an ugly mentality, devoid of basic human decency, that can be found throughout the various strata of society.

Class doesn't come into it – such obnoxious individuals don't have any, whether they're posh or poverty-stricken. And I try to avoid using divisive old-school class labels anyway; strongly believing we should all be equal.

Fiercely individual with a variety of skills and applications, maybe even different levels of wealth up to a point, but all treated with the same degrees of consideration and respect.

Having said that, it's a weird quirk of the Kyle show that most of the dreadful specimens featured do appear to be from more deprived neighbourhoods. Many of them are on benefits.

And that's why I felt the need to clarify my phrase in the song lyric, before people went off with the wrong impression.

It would have applied regardless of the social standing of the horrible and clearly unbalanced idiots washing their dirty linen in public.

January 27 – About 300 Auschwitz survivors are gathering at the site of the former Nazi death camp today to mark the 70th anniversary of its liberation by the Soviets.

The commemoration is taking place at the notorious site in southern Poland where more than a million people, mostly Jews, were exterminated between 1940 and 1945.

It's a deeply poignant occasion, made even more significant by the new rise in extreme right wing groups across Europe and various atrocities recently attributed to bloodlust Islamic fundamentalists.

I find it very, very scary that, seven decades on, the brutal and oppressive Nazi mentality is still alive, well and actually thriving on the violent fringes of religious and political thought across the board.

LET'S GET A LITTLE LOVE IN HERE
Martin Money, (written June 1976, revised October 2012)

Let's get a little love in here
Get a little love in here
We all need it – now ain't that clear? –
So let's get a little love in here.

In other news, Saudi King Abdullah bin Abdul Aziz has died aged 90, to be replaced by his brother Salman. The country is the world's biggest oil exporter.

Other recent deaths have included Swedish-born film star and one-time sex symbol Anita Ekberg, chart-topping Greek singer Demis Roussos and former Tory Home Secretary Leon Brittan.

On a lighter note, happy birthday Jake Yarwood, my buddy Steve's son. Have a good one, mate – and thanks for fixing my computer more than once!

January 29 – A friend of mine put a great Jimi Hendrix quote on Facebook today. It went "when the power of love overcomes the love of power, the world will know peace." I like that; it's really cool – and so true.

Speaking of quotes, a line in my recently-composed lyric No Woman I Know poses a question – can tigers change their stripes, or leopards their spots even?

My immediate reply in the same verse was an emphatic and pessimistic "no way!"

But I was making a point and in truth nothing's quite that clear-cut.

Sadly, the assertion does seem to be right more often than not, but it is possible for people to change as their own positive or negative energy streams win the inner fight.

In fact, most of us spend our whole lives switching from good to bad and back again with alarming speed in reaction to our experiences and circumstances.

A few seem to get stuck for long periods in one mode or the other and these people are regarded as either saints or monsters depending on which stream has prominence.

We all have inbuilt destructive traits but some are better at controlling them than others, that's all. And our levels of success or failure in this can fluctuate without warning. Demeanour and behaviour can be altered, basic character traits can't.

All we can do is try to moderate them as best we can. Some folk are more diligent in this than others.

January 30 – Mad prats make terrible bedfellows.

February 1 – Mosques across the country are opening their doors to the general public today in a bid to promote religious harmony and dispel negative ideas about Islam. How good is that?

People are being offered tea and cake and a chance to chat in a spirit of acceptance and mutual respect.

Similar initiatives are being or have been carried out in other countries including Germany and Australia.

The move follows the recent terror attacks in Paris and elsewhere said to be the work of Islamic extremists.

What a wonderful idea! I'm all for a bit of positive, peaceful bridge building to combat the destructive and divisive actions of unhinged zealots inflicting murders and mayhem.

Most Muslims despise the violent lunatic fringe groups that give their faith a bad name, just as most Christians strive to distance themselves from hard liners with fire and brimstone quotes, arrogant and intolerant attitudes and harmful sexual hang-ups.

Ey-up! Another new lyric has come to mind in the past couple of days. Here it is:

Martin Money, January 30 – February 1, 2015

Staying out of trouble is a full time job for you
Tempting though it is to slip some poison in the stew
Lovers or fierce rivals – makes no diff'rence in your mind
When you get the urge to be destructive or unkind

What is it that drives you to cause friction and alarm?
Why are you so prone to spread division, pain and harm?
Is it something others did that makes you burn and bruise?
Do your scars run deep? Well I'm afraid that's no excuse

This may seem harsh but it's the stone cold truth –
Oh no, there's no excuse
No excuse, no excuse
Oh no there's no excuse
People won't accept such things
Oh no, there's no excuse

Living with the actions of a wrecker isn't good
Try a little harder to resist – you know you should
Life would be much better if you tempered your desires
And fought your crazy impulse to start arguments and fires

What is it that drives you to cause friction and alarm?
Why are you so prone to spread division, pain and harm?
Is it something others did that makes you burn and bruise?
Do your scars run deep? Well I'm afraid that's no excuse

This may seem harsh but it's the stone cold truth –
Oh no, there's no excuse
No excuse, no excuse
Oh no there's no excuse
People won't accept such things
Oh no, there's no excuse

There's mischief in your bloodstream
There's malice in your heart
Where others join together
You just have to pull apart

When I started writing today's journal entry earlier on, I was listening to a CD of the best of Blondie. What a great band Debbie and the boys are – and still gigging. They played a great set at Glastonbury last summer that I watched again when it was repeated on BBC television last week.

After having a break for lunch, I'm now back at the computer keyboard to finish off this chapter. I've got the telly on now and ITV Three are repeating an episode of the star-studded Miss Marple series featuring Geraldine McEwan as Agatha Christie's world-famous amateur sleuth.

It's very topical in a sad and moving sort of way because Geraldine died two days ago aged 82. She had been ill after suffering a stroke back in October.

It's quite weird watching a TV programme while aware that its main star has so recently shuffled off this mortal coil. RIP Geraldine, you were good.

****

CHAPTER THREE – WHERE'S THE LOVE?

February 3, evening – History was made today as Parliament gave a resounding thumbs-up to a new scientific technique that allows babies to be created using the DNA of three people rather than two.

MPs in the Commons were given a free vote on the controversial issue with far-reaching moral and ethical implications. They backed the idea by 382 votes to 128.

Cutting-edge technology uses a modified version of IVF to combine the DNA of the pre-natal baby's two parents with the healthy mitochondria of a donor woman.

It's a move that could prevent children being born with health problems including brain damage, muscle wastage, heart failure and blindness.

Mitochondria are the tiny compartments inside nearly every cell of the body that convert food into useable energy.

Many will welcome this as a way of preventing youngsters from having heartbreaking and possibly life-threatening conditions, leading ultimately to a healthier populace.

But others, particularly those with religious convictions, see it as "playing God" while taking a sinister stride towards a genetically modified human race. There are also concerns over the safety and efficiency of the process.

Me? – I'm undecided. On the face of it this appears to be an exciting, significant, life-enhancing and even life-saving development. But I remain sceptical and very anxious over how such scientific advances can be used for far less altruistic purposes.

It begs the massive question – what type of society do we envisage in the future?

Speaking of which, I've been reading some updated parts of a website I referred to in my last book, *Diamonds and Gold*.

It's apparently been put into the public arena by the Illuminati, the group largely suspected of being the puppet-masters controlling the world from the shadows with a view to keeping all the wealth and power for their own privileged elite, regarding the rest of us as little more than expendable slaves to be used and abused.

But this website, claiming to be the work of the vilified group itself, asserts that the conspiracy theorists have it all wrong, and they're actually the good guys battling against that nasty elite which their enemies have misled people into thinking is them.

And those enemies are the all-powerful rulers and eager devotees of the corrupt, unfair and oppressive old world order they are determined to overthrow.

It's a system based on cruel capitalism, evil religions and sham democracy that they want to replace with a new world order – a meritocracy built on equality and justice.

The American, French and Russian revolutions were all started by right-minded pioneers with this commendable idea of how things should be, they claim.

The centrepiece of this new, fairer society would be a new type of human being – more advanced, enlightened and divine, fully aware of its own inner god status.

Christianity, Islam, Judaism and other religions reliant on grovelling subservience to a tyrannical deity would go, along with capitalism and elitism as a radical change in hearts and minds swept in a new golden age of human evolution bringing genuine fairness, they say.

A lot of this sounds spot on to me and I can fully support much of what the website authors are saying. But I'm deeply worried by their clinical, quite brutal approach where cold mathematics, science and reason replace compassion, warmth and soul.

I'm all for replacing privilege and nepotism with a set-up where the best qualified get to run things, regardless of their social background. But I'm very concerned that both democracy and the family unit could be casualties of this bold new vision.

I have a nagging feeling in my gut that such a vision smacks of the harsh, Darwinian survival-of-the-fittest ethos which can so easily be twisted to fit an agenda where the final destination is a nightmare cul-de-sac of ethnic cleansing and Nazi death camps.

And David Icke, one of the Illuminati's most famous critics, alleges the website's a smokescreen put out to spread lies and confusion while the evil group continues with its mission to tighten its selfish control over all the money, resources and power.

Well he would say that, wouldn't he, but he's bonkers, some would no doubt counter.

For myself, I'm convinced there's a ruthless, self-serving elite in charge of our planet but I don't know whether it's the Illuminati or another network.

I can find much to applaud on the website, no matter who's behind it. But I have severe reservations about where such thinking could lead us if enforced too viciously.

And I see the new DNA process as a double-edged sword, much like most new scientific breakthroughs.

Yes, it could reduce people's torment and culminate in a healthier, happier society – a double positive result.

But it could also be employed as a stepping stone to manipulating humans from birth. Messing with the contents of our food, drugs and water and planting microchips and other little technological wonders in newborns could – and I stress could – be others.

And, despite their obvious advantages, CCTV cameras, computers and the internet can also be used far too effectively to exploit and control us.

We live in a high-tech reality for sure – definitely a mixed blessing. And the cold and clinical way some people think and speak leads me to ask – where's the love?

February 4 – It's World Cancer Day so I've lit a candle and put a tribute on Facebook to victims of this far too commonplace killer disease that's taken many members of my family and countless others.

February 5 – Economic meltdown, climate change and social crisis. Sound familiar?

This could very well be a pretty accurate summary of the way things are right now. But in fact it's a brief description of Britain 3,000 years ago, as portrayed in a telly documentary I'm planning to watch tonight.

Amazing, innit? The older I get, the more I realise that, technological advances and a wafer-thin coating of so-called civilisation aside, very little we encounter in our 21st century existence is actually all that new.

February 6 – Birthday greetings go out to my friend Matt Brandt, a Bell regular. Have a blinder, mate!

I'm sporting a red tee-shirt and matching socks today as part of national campaign to raise awareness of life-threatening cardiac conditions and attract donations to the British Heart Foundation's research into ways of combating them.

You may well have seen recent TV adverts publicising Wear Red Day.

People who know me or have read my books will appreciate just how close to my own heart this issue is – sorry, just couldn't resist that highly appropriate pun!

Oh, by the way, I am of course wearing other clothes as well today – it's decidedly chilly out there, plus I don't want to be arrested!

Talking of charity fund-raising events reminds me of Live Aid, one of the biggest ever. I would have loved to attend the London concert, and would certainly have tried to get tickets had I not been otherwise occupied at another special occasion.

Imagine – Paul McCartney, David Bowie, Elton John, U2, Queen, the re-formed Who and a host of other rock and pop stars on the same bill. And all for a very worthy cause – relieving a devastating famine in Ethiopia.

When it was announced that hit making singer/songwriter/guitarist Julian Lennon, John's son, was also appearing the speculation machine went into overdrive.

Would George and Ringo take part? Was a Beatles reunion really on the cards with Julian taking his deceased dad's place? Wow – now that truly would make it a sensational show!

Event organiser Bob Geldof later revealed in his autobiography that the Beatles angle was a red herring and a complete non-starter because both Harrison and Starr had declined to participate. But at the time he refused to deny the possibility because it was five-star publicity for his charity money spinner.

Poor Julian felt so pressurized and weighed down by the frenzied media circus that he ended up pulling out of the London concert.

But the Who reformation (with Kenney Jones replacing the deceased Keith Moon) did take place at the Wembley Stadium show, along with reunions of both Led Zeppelin and Black Sabbath with Ozzy at a Live Aid concert in the States the same day.

Bob Dylan, Eric Clapton, Mick Jagger, the Beach Boys, Simple Minds and Madonna were also on the bill of the American show in Philadelphia.

And there were to be satellite link-ups between the two venues and others taking part in the fast-snowballing "global jukebox" event for the Ethiopians.

Wembley Stadium, Saturday July 13, 1985 – oh yes, that was definitely a date for our diary – my fiancée Joe and I, that is. But hang on, it already was.

Joe's twin sister Cheryl was marrying my mate Peter that day in Salisbury. And Joe was chief bridesmaid. So attending the Live Aid show was not an option.

My solution to this problem was to buy 4 four-hour video tapes and ask my mate Tom to record the whole 16 hours off the telly for me, taking in both the London and Philadelphia events.

He readily agreed, and when he and his wife Christine went out that evening – to the Home Guard social club I think – he asked their baby-sitter Vera to keep an eye on the recording session.

And Vera, bless her, came up trumps, even negotiating the TV channel switch from BBC One to BBC Two at 10pm as the London show ended and full coverage of the States concert began.

Vera, who has since passed on, was our drinking pal Andy Bethune's mum – a lovely lady.

Thanks to her, Tom and Chris, I ended up with the entire Live Aid spectacular on video. I still have the tapes but I no longer possess a video player. I can, however, watch the music marathon's highlights on four DVDs I also own.

Just in case you were wondering, yes we did give a donation to the charity.

And the wedding was a great occasion, as was our own the following year. Sadly, neither marriage lasted, but at least three of us are okay. I still see the twins at family do's such as Harvey's party last month. Not sure about Peter, we lost touch ages ago.

February 9 – Birthday greetings go out to my mate Mark "Tich" Hemington and Emily's sister Rachel Cooper, who now uses the Facebook name Claire.

Mark, who loves singing, invited me through Facebook to his birthday bash at the Bell last night coinciding with the pub's weekly karaoke session.

What a fine Sunday evening it was too! Matt Brandt was also there, still celebrating his birthday weekend with his lady Dani Knight, plus quite a few other friendly faces.

People such as my pals John Gaynor, John Palmer, Clare Hayes, Kelly Adams, Becky Browning, DJ Ross Maslin, guv'nors Mark Evans and Laura Williams and barmaid Sam Lowney.

Others I know turning up included Dawn Lewis, Penny Williams and Gemma Whike. Good times!

February 10 – The TV news is telling us that a fresh wave of anti-Semitism is sweeping our fair land and other European neighbour countries.

Oh great! Not content with demonizing Muslims, bigoted nut jobs are now targeting Jews as well – again.

These are bad tidings indeed. An intolerant and ugly right-wing attitude is once again increasingly making its presence felt, just like it did seven decades ago when it culminated in Hitler's horrific Nazi death camps.

Extremists twisting Islam for evil political purposes, inflicting blood-drenched jihads and barbaric beheadings, are other examples of this savagely intolerant mindset.

Oh come on guys! – For goodness' sake, can't we just all get along?

Let's face, it, our sceptred isle is a multi-racial, multi-cultural tapestry of vivid colours and dazzling diversity. It's been so for centuries.

Surely we should have learnt by now how to live together in peace? Why the hell haven't we?

It both amuses and irritates me when people say our government and communities should look after the English rather than constantly pander to foreigners.

The reason it amuses me is it begs the obvious question – what on Earth is their understanding of the word English?

Often the ones making such comments mean white-skinned folk with at least a passing relationship with our Christian heritage or older home-grown pagan roots.

Deliberately or inadvertently, they confuse racial background with religious beliefs and carelessly lump all perceived outsiders together as equally despised targets of prejudiced rage.

A large influx of people from Eastern Europe in recent years due to lop-sided immigration rules has meant that Poles, Romanians, Latvians and others from those territories are just as unpopular as the Muslims widely but unfairly blamed for political extremists' bloodlust terror attacks.

A much-hated Polish person might indeed be a Muslim, but could just as easily be a Jew, a Roman Catholic or an atheist. And, although from a Polish background, they were quite possibly born here, making them as English as anyone.

And this, for me, is the true definition of English – anyone, yes anyone, born here, regardless of racial or religious, ethnic or cultural differences.

People from Polish backgrounds have resided here for a long, long time, as have others from all over the world whose parents, grandparents or earlier ancestors came here at some point in the past.

We have English-Polish communities, English-Chinese, English-Italian, English-Indian, English-Greek – you name it, we've got it.

And that's great, just so long as there's no sharp segregation from the wider population, leading to resentment.

The same is true of religion. Once upon a time England, Wales, Scotland and Ireland were regarded as primarily Christian. Primarily, but never exclusively. So this was the belief system taught in most schools and it had by far the most churches.

But Jews, Muslims, Hindus, Buddhists, pagans and atheists have long histories here too. We just seem to have a lot more of all of them now, plus more overt displays of their presence including temples, synagogues and other places of worship.

I've just had a rather facetious but very pertinent thought – Christianity didn't originate in England anyway, it was imported. If Jesus turned up unannounced at Dover today without the necessary papers, would he be welcomed with open arms or told to go back home?

It's a moot point that shows just how ridiculous this whole white Christian prejudice issue really is.

My irritation comes from realizing that unreasonable bigotry is alive and well and such narrow-minded, elitist thinking is still too damned prevalent in our society.

****

CHAPTER FOUR – LYRICAL PAST

February 11 – I've just had a thought about how I could use that rhyming couplet I came up with last month but couldn't find a way to develop into a full song lyric.

You remember the one? –

With lyrics so colourful, music so sweet
Those rock and roll poets make my life complete.

{Martin Money, January 20, 2015}

My brainwave involves combining it with a piece I wrote yonks ago called Just a State of Mind. Penned in May 1976, it's a similar homage to the music I love.

So I've decided to tidy it up, add a bit of fresh polish and link it with the 2015 snippet thus:

STATE OF MIND

Martin Money,
Written May 16, 1976 to February 11, 2015

It's not where you work or what you eat
The clothes you wear, shoes on your feet
Or where you live, how rich you are
How many rooms, what type of car
Or if you're black or if you're white
Or if you're slow or if you're bright
The games you play, the friends you meet
Or if your manner's sour or sweet

Rock's a state of mind
Music's colour blind
It's a state of, it's a state of, it's a state of mind

It's not if you smoke or if you drink
Or if you're prone to stop and think

The things you do, the words you say
Or how you act in work or play
It's not the hype, the frozen smile
Or selling songs to make a pile
How many discs your band has sold
It's what you feel, not what you're told

Rock's a state of mind
Music's colour blind
It's a state of, it's a state of, it's a state of mind

With lyrics so colourful, music so sweet
Those rock and roll poets make my life complete.

Right, now let's see what other old song words I can refurbish and insert here while I'm in the mood.

First off, I'm going to go back even further, to a lyric I wrote in 1973 and two I composed in 1975. Namely, these:

LOVE WHERE DID YOU GO?

Martin Money, April 21, 1973

The room which once resounded to the sound of our laughter
The sofa where we said goodbye upon that fateful day
The silence of the atmosphere
The thought that once you were here
I'm all alone and miss you dearly – love where did you go?

The fireplace holds such mem'ries of the plans we made together
The carpet, shades of blue, where a million tears are shed
The tears of new-found loneliness
Are echoed now in emptiness
As I recall each warm caress – oh! Love where did you go?

Love where did you go?
I'm hurt and sad, I'm going mad
Oh love, where did you go?

The curtains where the sun beamed in, a shadow of our passion
Are now drawn in the day to keep the sunlight out
The rain that now pours in my heart

Could never really let me start
To live again since your departure – love where did you go?

Love where did you go?
I'm hurt and sad, I'm going mad
Oh love, where did you go?

LOVE WAS HERE YESTERDAY

Martin Money, August 5, 1975

Flowers once kissed by sun
Smelled so sweet, gave off heat –
The nat'ral kind

Songs of praise, childhood days
Younger blood then the flood
Submerged our minds

Love was here yesterday – or was it the day before?
All is lost, seems the cost
Don't matter any more

Apathy on a spree
Affluence killing sense
Of a richer life

Cross of gold turned so cold
Feels like lead feelings dead
In this place of strife

Love was here yesterday – or was it the day before?
All is lost, seems the cost
Don't matter any more.

WALL OF CONFUSION

Martin Money, May 31-June 1, 1975

The precinct stinks of petrol fumes which choke the gasping air
A solid wall of flesh and bone assaults me on the stair

The people, cushioned in their cells, ignore the world outside
The kids, the wife, the house, the car – "shall we have roast or
    fried?"

Seems to me they're deaf and blind
Keyed up brains that can't unwind
Crammed with useless information
Conscious of their own location
Am I like them or is it in my mind?

They flit around like brainless flies, their nerves like shredded
*   string*
I can't accept this pantomime of which I write and sing

Seems to me they're deaf and blind
Keyed up brains that can't unwind
Crammed with useless information
Conscious of their own location
Am I like them or is it in my mind?

Now on to December 1980 and other song words leading up to 1999:

LOVE YOU TOO MUCH

Martin Money, December 30 – January 1, 1981

I need you far more than you need me
I love you so much I can't tell
I want you to hurry on back now
Without you I'm living in Hell

I miss you so bad I can't tell you
I'm needing the warmth of your touch
I'm craving the joy that you gave me
Don't say that I'm asking too much
Guilty as charged – I've got you on the brain, seems I'm half
*   insane*
Writhing here in pain – Don't say it's all in vain
Please come back and tell me you feel the same
Coz I can't cope with this

I want you beside me forever
To share all my laughter and blues
But if you don't come back real fast babe
You leave me no choice what to do
Coz I can't live without you.

FLASHPOINT

Martin Money, September 7–11, 1985

Well I'm a regular guy in a regular mould
Don't ask for much, don't dig for gold
On the surface, yeah, I'm a peaceful soul
But don't push me, don't push me to flashpoint

Well I used to fight my way through life
But now I've got a house and wife
I've settled down, don't want no strife
But don't push me, don't push me to flashpoint
Flashpoint, flashpoint, backlash point
Don't push me, don't push me to flashpoint

Well, I'm a tough city blade who's got no hope
On the scrapheap of life, it ain't no joke
Just killing time till the bomb explodes
And they push me, they push me to flashpoint.

WAITING FOR SOMETHING TO HAPPEN

Martin Money, May 6–10, 1987

Is it the end of an era?
Is it the end of the line?
Is there a light round the corner? –
Fresh new horizons to shine?

Lost at the foot of the rainbow
Fading from splendour to grey
Stuck in a rut of indiff'rence
Nothing of value to say

And I'm waiting, yes I'm waiting
For something to happen

Can't see a rhyme or a reason
Can't see a purpose or cause
Why can't I do something useful?
Better my own life and yours?

Can't see the point
Of this mundane grind
Must find a way
To relieve my mind
I want to quit this job
Find a way to give
Make this crazy world
A better place to live

But I'm waiting, yes I'm waiting
For something to happen.

LAST ON THE LIST

Martin Money, May 12–13, 1987

Gas meter lovers stuck in a hovel
Coin crazy system sure makes 'em grovel

Newspaper cutting – hope springs from nowhere
New social housing – must try to go there

But they're last on the list, not a hope in Hell
As the lucky get homes in the pits they dwell

While a cash dazzled builder with a thousand schemes
Sends a bulldozer crashing through our rural dreams

They're still last on the list, not a hope in Hell
As the lucky get homes in the pits they dwell

Small giro victims, town centre madness
Cold country butcher fills me with sadness

And they're last on the list, not a hope in Hell
As the lucky get homes in the pits they dwell.

February 12 – And some more, spruced up and amended today:

TIRED

Martin Money, March 1–10, 1988

All dried up
All cried out
No tears left to weep
Dumb and dazed
Numb and lost
Walking in my sleep

The flood of words is a trickle now
I've gotta get it back somehow
But I'm tired, so damned tired

Vision's gone
Mission's end
Cannot see the light
Nothing rhymes
Nothing works
Lost the will to fight

The flood of words is a trickle now
I've gotta get it back somehow
But I'm tired, so damned tired

Older head
Colder heart
Sharp reality
Splintered faith
Hint of hate
Lost humanity

The flood of words is a trick now
I've gotta get it back somehow
But I'm tired, so damned tired.

HOOK, LINE AND SINKER

Martin Money, March 9, 1988

Hook, line and sinker
Baby, I fell for you
I'm a lucky guy

Feeling ten feet high
In the light of a love so true

When you broke the silence
Bringing colours to my sight
You healed my heart, restored my soul
And it happened overnight

Girl you gave me someone
To believe in instantly
The cynic's ice began to melt
In the warmth of honesty

Hook, line and sinker
Baby, I fell for you
I'm a lucky guy
Feeling ten feet high
In the light of a love so true

When the storm clouds gather
You can chase those blues away
And if I'm feeling sad and lost
You can brighten up my day
If the thunder cracks and rumbles
And the lightning strikes around
I can always shelter from the rain
In this sweet refuge I have found

Hook, line and sinker
Baby, I fell for you
I'm a lucky guy
Feeling ten feet high
In the light of a love so true.

THE STRANGER'S REFLECTION

Martin Money, June 6–12, 1988

Too long in the tooth
Too short of breath
Too long in the groove
And bored to death

Stranded up a creek
Without a prayer
Spirit's getting weak
You've had your share

You look in the mirror only to see
The reflection of a stranger

Man' you've left your tree
You've lost your punch
And it's plain to see
You're out to lunch

Staring like you've come
From outer space
Feeling bruised and numb –
So out of place

You look in the mirror only to see
The reflection of a stranger

Too long in the tooth
Too short of breath
Too long in the groove
And bored to death

Stranded up a creek
Without a prayer
Spirit's getting weak
You've had your share

You look in the mirror only to see
The reflection of a stranger.

THE EASY WAY OUT

Martin Money, Dec 11–21, 1990

I'm flying by the seat of my pants
Sailing close to the breeze
Cutting corners, taking chances
Not so keen to please

I'm racing to the edge of the world
Staring life in the face
Sick and tired of treading lightly
Keeping in my place

There was a time, not long ago
Caution was my code
Scared to blot my copy book
Loath to leave the road
But lately I've been thinking
Is it worth the fight?
Toeing someone else's line
Coz they say it's right?
So I'm taking the easy way out

Yes I'm flying by the seat of my pants
Sailing close to the breeze
Cutting corners, taking chances
Not so keen to please

And I'm setting my dials for the sky
Shaking loose from these chains
Breaking doors down, tasting freedom
From the stress and strains

Who are you to criticise –
Say I've got too slack
Just because I've found the way
To dodge a heart attack
And I'm taking the easy way out
Taking the easy way out
Had enough of stupid rules
I'm taking the easy way out

There was a time, not long ago
Caution was my code
Scared to blot my copy book
Loath to leave the road
But lately I've been thinking
Is it worth the fight?
Toeing someone else's line
Coz they say it's right?
So I'm taking the easy way out.

THE BEST THING THAT HAPPENED TO ME

Martin Money, January 2–11, 1991

There's stresses and strains of the monet'ry kind
The pressure at work's leaving scars on my mind
I'm battered and bruised, but babe I ain't blind
You're the best thing that's happened to me

As everyday life makes me sweat, swear and shout
I blow hot and cold as I'm rushing about
I don't often say this, but girl there's no doubt
You're the best thing that's happened to me

The best thing, the best thing, the best thing that's happened to me

My nose has been bloodied, my eyes have been blacked
It's hard to survive with your senses intact
But darlin' I'm always aware of the fact
You're the best thing that's happened to me

There's stresses and strains of the monet'ry kind
The pressure at work's leaving scars on my mind
I'm battered and bruised, but babe I ain't blind
You're the best thing that's happened to me

The best thing, the best thing, the best thing that's happened to me
The best thing, the best thing, the best thing that's happened to me.

JAGGED GLASS

Martin Money, September 4 – November 5, 1996

I was a lonely man with my telly, tunes and girlie magazines
Till you came along and reminded me just what good loving means

But there was a price 'coz I fell for you even though you told me no
Now I'm lost in time, strung out in space, deep in love – it hurts me
  so

But I thank you for bringing me alive
Yes I thank you for helping me survive
Even though you're tearing me apart
I say from the bottom of my broken heart

Thank you, still thank you

And I will not heed the jagged glass of reason so unkind
Though you love me back it's a diff'rent way and it really blows
*   my mind*

But I thank you for bringing me alive
Yes I thank you for helping me survive
Even though you're tearing me apart
I say from the bottom of my broken heart
Thank you, still thank you

I NEED TO KNOW

Martin Money, February 27–28, 1999

I'm a troubled guy who needs to know
Should I persevere or should I go?
I need to know your answer soon
You're my heart's desire, my sun and moon
I need to know girl, I need to know

And I'm trying hard to make it plain
You're my fireside glow and my summer rain
I need to know if there's a chance
For you and me and fine romance
I need to know girl, I need to know

Give me an answer to my plea
Babe put me out of my misery
I need to know, yes I need to know

If I'm way off course on a wild goose chase
Can you tell me now so I don't lose face?
I need to know your answer soon
You're my heart's desire, my sun and moon
I need to know girl, I need to know

Give me an answer, set me free
Babe put me out of my misery
I need to know.

One Day We Could Look Back and Laugh

Martin Money, March 5, 1999

I saw you in the street today – embarrassing surprise!
I blushed bright red and walked on fast, my mind was paralysed
I couldn't find the words to say or look you in the eye
It never used to be like this – I'm such a stupid guy!

One day we could look back on this and laugh

It's all my fault for sending you that Valentine on card
You took it bad and froze me out, poured ice upon my heart
I didn't mean to cause offence, my sentiments were true
But now you won't give me a chance to tell all this to you

We used to get on well but now we're more like enemies
I hate the silence and the way it's all turned out like this
We might end up together or we might end up apart
But please can we be friends at least and make a fresh new start?

One day we could look back on this and laugh.

And that just about wraps up this delve into my lyrical past and Chapter Four of this book.

****

CHAPTER FIVE – CATCHING THE YETTIES

February 13 – Today marks the 70th anniversary of the Allies' bombing of Dresden – a poignant reminder that it's not only nasty Nazis and violent radical Islamists who cause multiple deaths and mass destruction.

Tens of thousands of civilians were killed as the German city was devastated by a firestorm created by American and British aeroplanes.

Kinda makes what I actually sat down to type very pertinent indeed. Namely, this…

Having read all my so-far published books (*Sunshine and Ice Volumes One* to *Seven*), my very dear friend Carole Jones asked if I'd seen a BBC film called *Bitter Lake*.

I hadn't, but her question spurred me to try and seek it out, and using my computer I found and watched it last night on BBC iplayer. Carole was right – it blew me away.

I'd thoroughly recommend it to any thinking person who rejects the politicians' deliberately simplistic good versus evil bullshit regarding fierce ideological clashes.

The two hour-plus documentary is the work of award-winning film maker Adam Curtis and tells the unfolding story of power politics and religious fanaticism through the experiences of one country – Afghanistan.

He explains that the raging ideological and cultural war that's engulfing the world has its roots in history and is nowhere nears as straightforward as good guys versus bad guys, as the politicians would have us believe.

It's all here – Saudi Arabian oil, savage versions of Islam, false and perverse Western dreams of democracy and freedom, Israeli-Arab tension, the Gulf Wars, political chicanery, Iraq, Pakistan, the opium trade, the horror of 911, stock market crashes, cynicism, ambition, corruption and naïve but lethal visions of religious idealism.

I ended up feeling sorry for the poor Afghan innocents; British and American soldiers and equally earnest but misled and exploited Islamic purists caught up in the madness.

All have been mercilessly used in others' brutal and blood-drenched quests to gain and keep money and power. And I find that twisted, sickening and abhorrent.

In truth there's good and evil on both sides of the ideological barrier – honest, decent people who think they're doing the right thing and despicable bastards hell-bent on using that conviction to their own selfish ends.

This informative, enlightening but deeply unnerving and infuriating film proves once and for all what many of us knew already – politics most certainly is a very dirty business, devastating in the hands of the unscrupulous.

And it begins to answer a question I've already posed more than once – what drives young Muslims in this country to join radical Islamic groups and turn to violence?

Cheers Carole, you're a star – thanks to you, I have more food for thought. And I urge others to check out this amazing but deeply unsettling BBC film.

Spread the word, guys. And spread the love. Don't let the hate mongers, power freaks and vicious money-heads win. They've had it their own way for far too long.

Speaking of which, there's a general election in May.

February 15 – A ceasefire has just been declared in the Ukraine. Good – I hope it's the first step to a peaceful resolution of that country's problems and an end to the bitter fighting that's been tearing it apart.

Meanwhile, in Denmark, police say they've shot dead a gunman they believe was behind two deadly attacks in Copenhagen.

We're told that armed officers killed the man in the Norrebro district of the Danish capital after he opened fire on them.

It came after the two gun incidents yesterday – the first at a free speech debate in a café and the second near the city's main synagogue.

One person died and three police officers were injured at the café and a Jewish man was killed and two officers wounded in the later attack.

So, just like in France recently, ethnic violence and a bitter hatred of free speech have brought death to a capital city. Where's next – London, Berlin, Madrid, Vienna? Or maybe Amsterdam, Prague, Stockholm or Rome?

For it seems no-one's safe these days from the lethal actions of bloodlust political crazies with dangerously warped religious ideas.

Their attitudes are chillingly brutal and their methods disgustingly savage. They want to replace one seriously warped, deeply damaging system with an even more despicable one of savagely intolerant doctrine and undemocratic, vicious control.

And as a democrat who believes in tolerance, peace, harmony and freedom of speech and expression, that deeply offends my sense of justice and decency. It also scares the crap out of me.

But I'm just as angry at the existing set-up where cash is king and justice, compassion and any trace of spirituality are jettisoned in a frenzied drive for materialistic profit.

Speaking of which, I've found more Adam Curtis documentaries on the internet using my computer. Several have been blocked – I wonder why! – But the other four that remain accessible are in a BBC mini-series called *The Mayfair Set*.

Basically, they expand some of the themes of *Bitter Lake* – and particularly the apparent total surrender of political power on a global scale to ruthless and unscrupulous money-heads since the end of the Second World War.

This is precisely the outrageously unfair, brutal and corrupt capitalist system that Islamic extremists detest and are so keen to overthrow.

Catholic or Protestant or Muslim, Jain or Jew
What's the use of talking God while killing as you do?
(Love Burn the Ice, Martin Money, January 5–7, 1977)

I've done various jobs within that capitalist system in my time. And hated most of them. Okay, they've all had moments of pleasure, but all tolled they've added up to years of misery.

My own fault of course – I should have been much more focussed and determined in pursuing my dream of spending my time and earning my money writing prose and verse on my own terms, no-one else's.

But my quarter-century as a journalist did have some benefits. It paid the bills – well, sort of. It honed my writing style. It gave me a wider experience of the world around me. And it meant I saw loads of great rock and pop concerts for free and met several famous people.

One of those meetings, with Motorhead front man Lemmy, turned out to be life-changing, as mentioned in *Volume Six, Scratched Crystal*.

Other high points in the decades of hassle and unpleasantness included covering events such as Knowl Hill Steam Fair and Christchurch Folk Festival.

The steam fair was a weekend event at a village out in the country between Maidenhead and Reading. It was the seventies, during my time on the Maidenhead Advertiser.

And it was one of those wonderful occasions that stimulated al five senses at the same time.

The sight and feel of those lovely old engines, the sounds of the steam organs and the traditional fairground, the smells of coal, oil and burger vans, the taste of the take-away snacks and candy floss – oh yes, a sensual treat if ever there was one.

Covering it was hard work but thoroughly enjoyable, a nice break from the drudgery of the bulk of my labours as a local newspaper reporter.

The same was true of the folk festival, which I covered several times while reporting for the *Christchurch Times*.

Folk dancers in their colourful national dress came from all over Europe to appear alongside the English Morris men, singers and groups that took over the town's various halls and pubs and its picturesque Priory and castle grounds.

Some people hate Morris dancing, seeing it as old-fashioned, twee and decidedly effeminate. But one year the performers gave their display in the town hall because it was raining heavily outside – and it was quite an eye-opener, I can tell you.

Watching the Morris men close up indoors, I realised how physically fit and tough they had to be, especially when leaping and clashing those wooden sticks with some ferocity. This was no activity for the feeble or faint-hearted!

I really liked the event's rootsy, laid-back feel and especially some of the musicians. A personal highlight was catching the excellent Yetties at a ceilidh in Twynham School Hall. Fabulous!

The trio, who wrote their own folk songs, named themselves after Yetminster, the Dorset village where they grew up.

They retired in 2011 and accordion player Pete Shutler died last year, but they can still be heard every Sunday on the radio, playing the theme tune to the omnibus edition of long-running serial drama The Archers, about life in a fictional rural community.

February 16 – I've been investigating further the content and impact of Adam Curtis's documentaries as available on the internet.

As I've said, we can watch *Bitter Lake* and the *Mayfair Set* mini-series. We can also view three six-minute films by him. But some of his other, more controversial work has been blocked, such as *The Power of Nightmares*, *The Century of the Self*, *Pandora's Box* and *The Living Dead*.

But we can get a glimpse of what he says in them through Canadian James Corbett, who runs a regular blog for the alternative press.

In one hour-long edition of his Corbett Report, he analyses Curtis's films and comes to the conclusion that, although there's much there meriting praise and discussion, the Englishman takes too much at face value.

For example, he accepts without question that Lee Harvey Oswald killed John Kennedy, and that Islamic fanatics were responsible for 911, two of the favourite topics for conspiracy theorists.

And Curtis seems to think that hard cash, not religion, is the main cause of cultural and ideological friction and conflict, whereas in fact members of the ruthless elite in charge of our world have so much money it actually means little to them.

Their real drug is power, pure and simple, and they're obsessed with protecting their own interests and the bloodlines of their families that have run the show for aeons, claims Corbett.

And he appears to at least entertain the ideas of paedophilia, satanic worship and human sacrifices being parts of the sinister elite's sick agenda.

In this, he's closer to David Icke's thinking than Adam Curtis's. I've yet to discover whether he goes as far as the admittedly bizarre shape-shifting reptilian aliens angle.

As you've probably gathered, I find all this stuff riveting but frightening as hell.

I keep an open mind to all possibilities and I'm convinced that the stark reality of what's actually going on is miles away from the official versions constantly put out by career-protecting politicians and a pathetically compliant media.

I also firmly believe that those in the know aren't telling us anywhere near the whole story.

Thanks to Carole, I've become an Adam Curtis fan. His is the type of investigative journalism that truly warrants the description.

He's bold, questioning and controversial, looking behind news bulletins and recorded history in an attempt to uncover the truth.

Okay, he's got his own views and can manipulate media reports to reflect them. But we all do this, all the time – use accepted facts in a way that helps us make our own points. We all have our own agendas, whether we admit it or not.

The only difference is that some are just a lot more evil and damaging than others.

This applies on a wide variety of scales from the small, where it involves family, friends and others we each mix and work with, right up to the global stage, where it applies to nations and major groupings.

And there have been agendas galore for ages in the Middle East, where Egyptian jets have today been bombing Islamic State targets in Libya.

The attack followed the release of a video showing the beheading of 21 Egyptian Christians by IS members.

So it's looking like Christians and Jews have been killed by Islamic extremists in recent weeks.

I repeat my lyrical question:

Catholic or Protestant or Muslim, Jain or Jew
What's the use of talking God while killing as you do?

The reference to Catholics and Protestants is an indicator that this verse was written back in 1977 when Northern Ireland was still being ripped apart by sectarian violence.

But no matter which religious grouping murderous meatheads claim to come from, their actions are still intolerable and wrong – just plain evil in fact.

February 17 – It's Pancake Day, or to apply its official name, Shrove Tuesday – the day before Ash Wednesday, the start of Lent.

Lent is the 40-day Christian fasting season leading up to Easter, this year being marked on the weekend of April 3 to 6.

Pancakes are associated with the day preceding Lent because they were a way to use up rich foods such as eggs, milk, and sugar before believers resorted to eating plainer fare, more associated with nutrition than pleasure, for the six-week period.

Some folk wonder why Easter moves every year yet Christmas is always December 25. The reason is Easter is governed by phases of the Moon – ironic, really, as the Moon is far more associated with paganism and other faiths than Christianity.

Another lyric has crystallized in my addled mind over the past couple of days – inspired by Adam Curtis and the search for truth.

It goes like this:

UNFOLDING TRUTH

Martin Money, February 16–17, 2015

It's all part of an ongoing story
All part of an unfolding truth
All part of solving the puzzle
All part of gathering proof

Each day we learn a little more about the world we live in
Our eyes are opened bit by bit to falsehoods we are given

Each time we read the morning press or watch the news at seven
We get a version of events and tales of Hell and Heaven

We have to go beyond that
We need to use our brains
To switch our bullshit filters on
And find out what remains

It's all part of an ongoing story
All part of an unfolding truth
All part of solving the puzzle
All part of gathering proof

Each year that passes makes us doubt what's fact and what is
*   fiction*
What's good and evil, right and wrong and who incites the friction

It's all part of an ongoing story
All part of an unfolding truth
All part of solving the puzzle
All part of gathering proof

Each day we learn a little more about the world we live in
Our eyes are opened bit by bit to the falsehoods we are given

Each time we read the morning press or watch the news at seven
We get a version of events and tales of Hell and Heaven

We have to go beyond that
We need to use our brains
To switch our bullshit filters on
And find out what remains

We all have those folk who make our skin crawl. Well-known faces having that effect on me include David Cameron, George Osborne, Nick Clegg, Jeremy Kyle, Gordon Ramsay, Katie Hopkins, Simon Cowell, Edwina Currie, Keith Lemon, Ann Widdecombe, Jeremy Clarkson, Nigel Farage and Harry Hill.

Rude, bad-tempered media people who interrupt, talk over or cut off interviewees also get my goat. So do all violent head cases, arrogant know-alls, ego-maniacs, racist or bigoted thugs, brutal bullies and self-obsessed habitual liars, thieves and deceivers.

Plus anyone who viciously abuses or exploits children, adults or animals.

Others will have different celebrities and types of individual they find obnoxious and repellent. There's a huge temptation to release our intense exasperation by demanding they're all nailed to trees in the New Forest. But there are two big problems with this.

Firstly, we'd probably run out of trees pretty damned fast. But more importantly, our very human and natural knee-jerk reaction would show that we're once again being sucked into the prevalent negative atmosphere of division and hatred.

At such times we need to pull ourselves up sharply – in my case trying to revert to peaceful hippy mode as quickly as possible.

Right, now I'm going to finish off today's journal entry and have some tea. Pancakes, of course – granted, higher in fat and sugar than the food I normally eat but what the heck, doesn't harm once in a while, does it, eh?

February 19 – By continuing my internet searches, I've managed to find my way around attempts to block Adam Curtis's films to view a few more of them.

They're all eye-opening and thought-provoking and their themes tend to overlap.

The Power of Nightmares (The Rise of the Politics of Fear) reveals how politicians and community leaders on all sides of bitter ideological divides have managed to convince people that their invented stories of serious threats are terrifyingly real.

The Century of the Self tells how Sigmund Freud's ideas have been used to maximum effect by advertisers and other thought manipulators to influence and control folk by appealing to their very self-centred but often subconscious desires.

Pandora's Box, *The Living Dead* and *The Trap* are also fascinating and alarming in equal measure. I'd recommend them all. Curtis is a champion of free thought in an age of smoke and mirrors, lethal propaganda and damaging indoctrination.

Changing the subject completely, two totally random and unconnected memories have surfaced in my mind in the past couple of hours or so.

The first dates back to my time as a local newspaper reporter in Christchurch and the second concerns an incident that occurred on one of my short stays in Liverpool.

A fellow journalist I used to work with in the Dorset town had a very pronounced and distinctly Scottish-sounding accent.

On first meeting him, no-one believed his claim to be English. We thought he was joking. But he was factually correct, being born and bred in Berwick-on-Tweed, a town in Northumberland just three miles this side of the border.

It's doubly confusing for those who know that Berwick Rangers are a Scottish league football team.

And my colleague's name? – Derek. Yep, Derek from Berwick, a friendly, jovial feller everyone liked And not Scottish at all.

My second memory involves my Liverpool mate Pat and a Saturday evening in one of the city's pubs.

Pat, sadly no longer with us, was Tom and Carole Jones' mum. I've previously told how I used to drive Tom, his lady Christine and sometimes his sister Carole up to Liverpool from Bournemouth every now and then to spend a week with Pat and her hubby Chris.

They welcomed me with open arms and Pat used to call me her little Pisces pal as we shared that star sign.

She and Chris were huge Everton football club fans so we'd spend Saturday nights in an Everton pub talking about the team's fortunes earlier that day amid booze-fuelled discussions and jokes spanning a whole range of subjects.

Rather than karaoke – then a quite new craze sweeping the country – the pub we used had open mike evenings where anyone could get up and sing with a live musical trio.

And there were some damned fine singers too – all amateurs such as dustmen, office workers and suchlike just having a good time on a night out.

There were also some very funny people capable of coming up with totally original and clever one-liners they'd just thought of. No wonder the city's produced so many top stars in the fields of music and comedy!

Anyway, this one evening three girls got up to sing with the trio. More than a bit tipsy, they launched into the Gerry and the Pacemakers classic You'll Never Walk Alone – quite well, actually.

Seeing me nodding my head in approval, Pat told me "don't you dare think of clapping them or we'll fall out – they're taking the mick, singing THAT song in an Everton pub!"

For anyone who doesn't know, You'll Never Walk Alone is a terrace favourite of Liverpool football club – Everton's close neighbour and arch rival.

This is one of many fond recollections of my times with members of the Jones family in Liverpool and Bournemouth. Happy days!

February 20 – I'm a passionate believer in the ideals of freedom and democracy. But that's exactly what they are – ideals to be strived for, not fully operational aspects of reality as we know it.

Granted, we have more of both in England than other parts of the world, but both are being eroded daily.

Our political leaders love to tell that we have an abundance of them, but this is a falsehood, a cleverly-orchestrated illusion.

In truth, both have been sacrificed in a mad quest for money and power where profit and loss, market forces and perceived economic prosperity are seen as paramount and it's all come down to numbers, formulae, criteria and equations.

We've all been handed on a plate to greedy bankers and ruthless business tycoons while unfeeling, clinical, rational computers have replaced the human touch in a system of government shaped by cold, stark statistics. It's all so superficial.

But those statistics can be cynically manipulated and figures vigorously massaged by the devious desperately driven to meet totally unrealistic targets or lose their jobs.

People have become little more than units, flesh and bone robots herded, controlled, exploited and frightened into compliance to a merciless administrative machine.

They're scared stiff by callous and reckless talk of outside threats, pandemic killer diseases, cancer and other lethal health issues, plus fears of drug and food side effects and the constant risks of losing everything, becoming destitute.

All this makes them so very vulnerable to manipulation and exploitation.

An explosion of psychological and psychiatric theories has been brought to bear on confused populations as a plethora of new buzzwords has left them wondering who the hell can be classed as completely sane and free of all mental health problems.

Drug companies have cashed in on this confusion and made fortunes through the prescription and sale of mind-altering pills such as Prozac, Rohypnol and Valium.

Corruption is rife in the corridors of power and it permeates through all sections of society. The media has largely become the politicians' public relations wing.

Individuals and groupings are encouraged to be ruthlessly self-serving at the expense of others' welfare. Community spirit and mutual support are viewed as the bleeding heart liberalism that's got us in this mess.

I fear the end result of all this will be a future ruled by a form of brutal fascism parading as democracy, couched in the language of patronizing platitudes.

Not content with screwing up their own countries, politicians try to export this twisted version of Western capitalism and impose it on other parts of the world – with disastrous consequences and in some cases violent backlashes.

Religious purists at home and abroad despair at this festering and crumbling edifice and yearn to get back to basics with something less corrupt, complex and confusing, more honest and spiritually satisfying.

I do I guess, but with the vital provisos that genuine democracy, grass-roots government, care for the environment, community spirit, mutual support, compassion, common sense and decency are all incorporated in a fresh new set-up.

Plus of course peace, harmony, freedom of speech and expression and tolerance of different faiths, ethnic and cultural backgrounds, sexual and political preferences.

But others, just as angered and disillusioned by the current situation, see a far more savage solution – forcibly imposing a stark, intolerant, viciously authoritarian system of tunnel-vision control where perceived offenders are brutalized and beheaded.

On balance, I think I'd much rather keep what we've got thank you – Deeply unsatisfactory and dreadfully flawed as it is.

But I do firmly advocate that we all try to work within it to radically improve things along the lines I've suggested rather than violently replace it with a different kind of nightmare.

Phew! – I think it's time to lighten up after all that serious stuff, don't you?

I find it so very cool that my son Phil shares my sense of humour and my tastes in quite a lot of things.

When he was a teenager, we used to have long conversations about TV programmes such as the Simpsons and Buffy and the Vampire Slayer and popular music stars from the Spice Girls to Linkin Park.

These days we're both huge fans of Family Guy, the satirical and sometimes wonderfully surreal American cartoon show. So when Phil saw a video clip of a camel laughing like its main character Peter Griffin, he tagged me on Facebook so I could check it out.

Okay, the clip was no doubt faked and the result of clever editing and dubbing, but that's not the point. It amused me greatly, just as Phil knew it would – and that's just fantastic!

It's also great how history tends to repeat itself when Phil and Emily come to visit, bringing my grandchildren.

Watching my son stroll along Fisherman's Walk to the seafront with them, feeding nuts to the squirrels and pausing by a small pond to see the fish, reminds me of those halcyon days that I used to do all those things with him when he was just a boy.

Quality father and son time – or in Chloe's case, daughter – is so very precious, don't you think?

One day last summer we all ended up down on the beach in the bright hot sunshine. As we left it to head back to mine, Phil, then 24, said: "Aren't you going to make me a car in the sand Dad, like you used to?"

It was a humorous and heart-warming moment, showing that he fondly remembers those wonderful times too. Sweet!

By the way, happy 50th birthday Alan Painter, one of the old Bell pub crowd back in the day. Have a golden day, mate!

February 23 – Movie land's glittering stars gathered at Hollywood last night for the 87th annual Oscars ceremony.

Englishman Eddie Redmayne, playing living legend science whiz Stephen Hawking in biographical production *The Theory of Everything*, was named best actor.

American Julianne Moore took best actress for her portrayal of a college professor suffering from Alzheimer's disease in the moving drama *Still Alice*

And *Birdman*, a black comedy starring Michael Keaton, was picked as best film.

Hmm – I've just used the term "glittering stars" for the second time in this book. Sounds like a nice overall title for it to me.

So from now on this will be known *as Sunshine and Ice Volume Ten – Glittering Stars*. Sorted!

February 25 – Happy birthday to me, happy birthday to me, happy birthday dear Martin, happy birthday to me. Yes, I'm 61 today but I don't feel a day over… 60.

I switched on my computer a short while ago to find that loads of friends had sent me Facebook messages, bless 'em. Makes you feel kinda warm inside, don't it?

Carol and David posted me a lovely self-made decoupage card and a fab Beatles Yellow Submarine tee-shirt. Suzette and Joyce each sent me cards with cash in them, which I'll spend when I go to Boscombe next Monday.

Cousin Sandra and her feller Alan also sent me a card. And my present to myself was an acoustic bass guitar picked up cheap in a second-hand shop. Can't play it yet but it will be fun trying to pick out the bass lines to classic rock tracks.

I'm having a quiet one today as I'll probably celebrate at the weekend – I'm off to Sam and Carl's on Friday and there's a rock band at the pub Saturday I want to see.

While typing this, I'm playing George Harrison's brilliant album All Things Must Pass and it's just reached the title song. The ex-Beatle would have been 72 today had he not passed on in 2001.

I watched American film maker Martin Scorsese's four-hour, two-part television documentary Living in the Material World again last night. I've got it stored in my Virgin TV On Demand library, having previously recorded it.

It's an affectionate but honest summary of the life of a guy who truly deserved the over-used title legend. And not just for his musical prowess and song writing skills.

He was kind, generous, funny, sensitive, perceptive, deeply spiritual and very wise – all virtues I attempt to emulate but could never get within a mile of his levels.

But, just like his great mate John Lennon, he could also be angry, abrasive, stubborn, thoughtless and cruel. He was as riddled with flaws and dark currents as any of us.

And yet his two former wives, his son and his many close friends accepted and embraced these imperfections because on balance he was a terrific force for good, a pretty special feller, deeply loved by all who knew him.

He was the sort of person I could listen to for hours – and I'm not just referring to the fantastic music he wrote and performed. I also mean the things he said in conversation and the sterling values he stood for.

Our modern world desperately needs men like George, John, Bob Marley and Jimi Hendrix – dazzlingly creative guys with great compassion and sound advice about how we should treat one another and what's really important in this crazy existence.

Yep, I know I bang on about it like a cracked Beatles record, but I'm talking once again about love and peace – man. Boy do we need both – more than ever!

February 26 – It was a special birthday treat for me to watch the Brit Awards live on telly last night.

I say treat, because it showed just how healthy our pop and rock scene is looking these days.

Okay, so I'm still waiting for the fresh and exciting new genre that's going to sweep all before it in an exhilarating burst of energy and invention.

But in the meantime there's some mighty fine artists around at the moment – people like Paloma Faith, named best British female. I'm playing her excellent album A Perfect Contradiction as I type this. It's modern soul at its very best – brilliant!

Then there's Ed Sheeran (best British male, best British album), Sam Smith (British breakthrough and British global success awards), Royal Blood (best British band) and Taylor Swift (international female) – all of them excellent.

And each of these acts put on a great one-song show in addition to picking up their prizes. Other live performers included Take That, Kanye West and Madonna, who took a nasty looking fall using stage stairs but carried on like the trooper she is.

Mark Ronson was given the best British single award, boy band One Direction took best video and singer-songwriter James Bay was most promising newcomer. The Foo Fighters were named best international band and Pharrell Williams, top global male.

None of the last five mentioned do that much for me even though I did have a lot of time for the magnificent Nirvana, Fighters front man Dave Grohl's former group.

Current favourites of mine who didn't win Brits this time around include Rita Ora, Ellie Goulding, Jake Bugg, Tom Odell, Clean Bandit, Calvin Harris, Katy Perry, David Guetta, Iggy Azalea, the Black Keys, Passenger, Avicii and Meghan Trainor.

Oh yes, there's a wealth of talent playing some great music out there and over the past six decades or so I've loved the work of many artists performing in a variety of styles.

But I remain very much a Beatles/Led Zeppelin/Pink Floyd guy at heart and always will be. All-time solo choices include Hendrix, Dylan, Marley, Kate Bush and Bowie.

February 27 – Stunned and enraged. That sums up how I was left feeling after witnessing an item on this morning's TV news.

It was about hospital A and E departments getting better at seeing patients within four hours, but still slightly missing a 95 per cent target figure.

FOUR SODDING HOURS?? That's disgusting, insane, barbaric and potentially lethal. Imagine if the fire service worked to the same guidelines.

"We've had a report of an explosion at a chemicals factory. Blaze out of control and spreading, 10 dead and 30 critically injured."

"Oh dear, that's a shame. Tell 'em we're a bit busy at the moment and ask them if they can wait till tomorrow."

I mean, the clue's in the ruddy name. A and E stands for Accident and Emergency – that is, urgent cases that need to been seen straightaway rather than going through the usual channels of consulting a GP then going to hospital if that's deemed necessary.

Anxious people, many of them in pain and some possibly dying, being forced to hang around that long to be treated says to me that something is very seriously wrong.

And it tells me we desperately need more and probably bigger A and E departments and extra trained staff to man them – the sooner the better.

I mean – It's hardly a new concept. Hospitals have had such supposedly fast-track emergency departments, once called casualty units, for ages. Their numbers, sizes and staffing levels should have kept pace with the demand for them without question.

Stuff the political arguments – surely its common sense and just plain common decency in a so-called civilised society? But apparently not.

By the way, the *Oxford English Dictionary* definition of a casualty unit is "the department of a hospital providing immediate treatment for emergency cases."

Exactly!

So now they've actually been renamed Accident and Emergency departments, it makes even more of a mockery of the description – a frigging travesty in fact.

I was very lucky when rushed to Poole Hospital after being assaulted at Christmas 2001. As I had a potentially life-threatening head injury, I was plonked in a wheelchair and whisked past the waiting crowds to be seen immediately.

It was indeed a significant wound and the whole ordeal had a profound and long-lasting impact on me, recorded in some detail in *Sunshine and Ice Volume Two* (*Descent into Darkness*). But it could have been a lot worse.

Thankfully, the over-stretched but alert medics saw this and acted upon it without hesitation. But in another, very similar but more serious case, the outcome could be tragic if the staff show less diligence and the injured person is made to wait too long.

I find that totally unacceptable – don't you? (If the answer's no, I'd start worrying!).

Granted, some people turn up unnecessarily at A and E because it's the only place open at night or over weekends when their usual doctor's surgery is closed.

But surely a brief assessment of each patient as they arrive would sort out the time-wasters and non-urgent cases from the more serious ones without too much delay.

Those needing hospital admittance or immediate treatment could then be dealt with in order of priority and the rest politely advised to contact their GP's surgery at the next available opportunity. And if they haven't got a GP, to sort one out pretty sharpish.

Blimey – It's not rocket science! And if it means more staff and bigger units, so be it. For pity's sake, screw this disgraceful four hours cobblers. Make it happen – now!

And before anyone questions the costs, may I point to the 40-plus billion put aside for the HS2 rail track, the massive expense of military hardware and adventures and the huge amounts scandalously withdrawn from benefit claimants, to name just three?

February 28 – Spock's gone to the stars. Yes, Leonard Nimoy, who played half-human half-alien Mr Spock in the *Star Trek* movies and TV shows, has died aged 83 from a chronic lung disease – even though he gave up smoking 30 years ago.

The actor and director shot to international fame in the global smash hit science fiction telly show, which spawned several spin-offs and a dozen feature films.

Spock will always be remembered for his catchphrases "illogical, Captain" and "live long and prosper", the second accompanied by a distinctive hand signal.

I'd like to wish a very happy birthday to my mates Gary "Gadget" Preston, John "Brun" Smith and Bell barmaid Tamzin Lee. They're all Facebook friends of mine so I've posted messages on their timelines.

As for my own belated birthday booze-ups, I went to Sam and Carl's yesterday as planned and they gave me a super wooden box incense stick holder and a chocolate cake from them and their family.

They also presented me with a greetings card that said "enjoy your birthday – at your age every second counts." Ha ha! – I like that, because it's funny but also very true, regardless of age.

My dear friend Carole Jones sent me a lovely happy birthday private Facebook message, bless her. And in all, I had over 40 items posted on my public timeline by family members and mates. Wow – I was moved. What a terrific bunch!

I'm off to the Bell tonight to continue my celebrations and also see Fired Up, a local rock band said to be very good.

March 1 – They were indeed very good and it was an excellent evening in the company of several friends including Jem Hannen, his nephew Stu and Stu's lady Melanie, John Gaynor, Ollie Okoye, Mark Hemington, Kelly Adams, Dawn Lewis, Penny Williams, birthday girl and barmaid Tamzin Lee and Bell guv'nors Laura Williams and Mark Evans.

Mark and Laura bought me a birthday beer, bless 'em, and so did Jem and John. All in all, it was a great night.

My excellent birthday weekend ended on a high note today when Phil and Emily came over with Harvey. (Lucas was with his mum and Chloe with Gail, Em's mum.)

Harvey handed me a "happy birthday" bag containing two cards, one from the children and the other from Phil and Emily, and a super tee-shirt bearing the humorous slogan "I'm too old for this shi(r)t!"

Ha ha! – talk about clever wordplay! I love it.

Their visit was the icing on the cake of a mighty fine celebratory few days. Sweet!

March 2 – Happy second wedding anniversary to Phil and Emily. Yep, two years ago today was one of the best days of my life – seeing my son marry his childhood sweetheart, the lovely Emily.

Happy birthday Jeanette Clough and Tara Seawright, two friends of mine who have each worked behind the Bell bar in the past.

March 3 – My dear sister Jan died three years ago today. I'm going to light a candle for her and put a little tribute on Facebook.

Sunshine and Ice Volume Four, Rosebeds and Dustbins/ Snow and Hatred, has been out exactly a year. A week from now, March 10, is the first anniversary of *Volume Five, A Twist of Fate,* and March 17 marks a year of *Volume Six, Scratched Crystal.*

I went to Boscombe yesterday to do a food shop at Sainsbury's, buy a few other bits and bobs and spend my birthday money from Suzette and Joyce.

I bought CDs by Sam Smith (In the Lonely Hour) and local rock group Galahad (Battle Scars) and a movie on DVD called *Dracula Untold – the Legend is Born.*

Oh Gawd here we go – the TV news channels are getting clogged up with speeches by top politicians fishing for votes as the build-up to the May general election intensifies.

It's a sickening sight and Cameron is predictably but infuriatingly persisting with his outlandish claim that our battered economy is on the road to recovery thanks to him and his cruel, cavalier cronies.

He clearly wants us to forget Osborne's threat of 14 months ago that if the Tories get back in they'll cut another £25 billion from government budgets, half from welfare.

Looks like the PM's keeping fingers crossed we have – so if voters with short memories are daft enough to return his dreadful crew to power, they can inflict further swingeing and spiteful cuts while countering any protests with "well we did tell you."

What a pity he's not talking quite so boldly about wielding the axe now he's pandering like mad and trying to come across as Saint David!

March 3 – four hours later – I watched my new Dracula DVD last night and I've just played my Sam Smith and Galahad CDs. I'd highly recommend them all!

A mate of mine put a great status on Facebook this morning asking the question "why do we talk of a highway to Hell but only a stairway to Heaven? – says a lot about anticipated traffic volumes!" Ha ha! – Excellent!

Like I've always said, not one of us is a complete angel so we should recognize our own flaws and foibles while cutting each other a heck of a lot more slack.

March 5 – I'm playing a Janis Joplin CD. Wow, what an amazing singer she was! Her searing vocals on Ball and Chain alone give her automatic admittance to the Rock and Roll Hall of Fame as far as I'm concerned.

But she could sing sweetly as well as belt them out and also wrote some of the songs she performed. People who saw her live described her stage presence as electric.

She's my third favourite female music star of all time, behind Kate Bush and Joni Mitchell, and just ahead of Dusty Springfield. And I consider that praise indeed!

Such a shame she died so young – just 27, supposedly of an accidental heroin overdose possibly intensified by alcohol.

Janis was once quoted as saying: "On stage, I make love to 25,000 different people, then I go home alone."

March 9 – I've just had a 24-hour blood pressure monitor fitted – one of those irksome things I have to do once a year now. I'm going back to the clinic in Boscombe tomorrow morning to have it taken off.

In the meantime I can't really do a lot – not that I do all that much nowadays at the best of times. So I'm going to chill.

To help in this, I'm playing a Tangerine Dream CD. Top-notch chill-out sounds or what?!

Actually, I've had quite an eclectic weekend music-wise – Janis Joplin on Friday, Billy Bragg Saturday, Leftfield yesterday and the dream-weavers today.

I've also watched the impeccable Matrix movie trilogy on DVD and various telly treats including Jane Eyre, Family Guy, the soaps, Russell Howard's Good News and A Touch of Frost.

Oh, and I went to Sam and Carl's for a booze and laughs session on Friday evening with them, Becca, Rudy, Bailey, Diane, Russell and Albert the dog.

Nice to mix it up a bit, don't you think?

Speaking of Billy Bragg, the lyrics to one of his older songs refers to the idea of property ownership being theft.

This is an old anarchist saying, later adopted by certain left-wing hard line socialists who feel that all land and buildings should be in the public domain and buying and using them for private purposes should be outlawed.

Such folk view such annexation as selfish, elitist, divisive and immoral, putting two fingers up to the rest of society.

The idealist in me wholeheartedly agrees with them but in truth nothing's quite that simple and I take the same attitude to land and property as I do money – I don't mind people having them, it's how much and what they do with them that's important.

Avariciously hoarding massive amounts of wealth and possessions is totally out of order and should be prevented by law.

At the other end of the scale, allowing people to be homeless and poverty-stricken should also be made illegal and help should given without question where it's needed to ensure it never happens.

But between the two extremes lie a whole spectrum of situations and a wide range of wealth levels.

And I feel as uneasy about the iron-fist, freedom-robbing anarchist/communist approach as I do the "I'm all right Jack, up yours" hard line capitalist mindset.

Even Bragg himself, an avid leftie, can appreciate that things aren't as black and white as we'd like them. He's always had a pragmatic streak and a witty sense of irony and self-deprecation, as evidenced in some of his songs.

That's why I like him – he seems a genuinely warm, funny guy who doesn't take himself too seriously, not some po-faced political bore hopelessly hung up on dogma and slogans.

And he does write and perform some bloody good stuff, full of catchy melodies, humour and perception.

Check out the words to Waiting for the Great Leap Forwards, for example. The idealism is tinged with cynicism and the wit has a sardonic twist. It ends with the declaration: "The revolution is just a t-shirt away." Superb!

Incidentally, there are two oft-misunderstood concepts involved in my comments of the last few paragraphs. One is anarchy and the other, property ownership.

Many people use the word anarchy as an alternative noun to chaos. I have in the past. But anarchy as a political idea means more self-government and less state control.

Advocates say we should run society through non-hierarchical organizations or voluntary associations.

Mainstream political parties warn that this would be a recipe for disaster, resulting in a fragmented, uncoordinated rabble incapable of running a tap let alone a country.

Well they would say that, wouldn't they? Those in power would lose their grip on it while others in opposition would have to kiss goodbye to any hopes of attaining it!

Yes, it could well result in chaos, a total lack of structure and cohesion, but it needn't. In practice, I fear it actually would, which is why I for one don't want to go that far.

But I do say we could try venturing part-way down that road, so to speak, by having more fluid and flexible, less structured and more grass-roots forms of government and a lot more of an each-case-on-its-merits, common sense method of working.

Decentralise government and hand the power back to the people at a more local level.

Far better that than what we've got now – a massive, too-rigid monolithic bureaucracy built around a pointless, soulless but lethal numbers game in which most players are obsessed with cold and harsh but scarily unreliable and interchangeable statistics.

It's all about profit and loss accounting, formulas, profiles, targets and other such superficial garbage at the expense of spirituality, compassion and human decency.

The other much-misunderstood and ruthlessly exploited term I want to highlight is property ownership. It infuriates me how much total crap is spoken about it.

In my book, a property owner is someone who's either paid off their mortgage or bought land or a building outright.

It certainly shouldn't be used to describe those who have landed themselves with colossal debts in order to live in their homes, facing the constant threat that defaulting on monthly payments would mean eviction and a building society taking possession.

If they truly owned the property, that couldn't happen. It would be theirs to keep or sell off if and when they wished – or leave to others in their will.

But politicians, especially Tory ones, love prattling on about living in a "home-owning democracy." The description is an affront to both parts of the phrase.

Of course they want people to have mortgages – that way, they're in their power, forced to toe the line and do as they're told through fear of losing everything. They become such easy prey for unscrupulous manipulators.

In other words, it means they're inextricably plugged in to the corrupt cash-mad capitalist set-up that the politicians and their overlords ruthlessly exploit in order to maintain control.

And that's why MPs and establishment top dogs give anarchy such a bad press. It's a major threat to them, you see.

Speaking as someone who once had a mortgaged home, full time job, car and all the other paraphernalia, I must say I'd much rather be in my current situation, a largely stress-free existence in private rented accommodation.

As the least practical man in the world, it suits me fine that when things go wrong in my flat it's my landlord's responsibility to get them fixed and at his expense not mine.

Okay, so I don't have bricks and mortar to my name – but neither do mortgage holders really – and I don't have the hassle, cost implications and downright dread involved in taking out a massive loan and paying my own maintenance bills.

So I couldn't really go with the "property is theft" argument too far, could I? My landlord, Barry, owns houses converted to flats that he rents out to people like me. He's providing a service – unlike the greedy who keep everything to themselves.

This is what I mean about how much people possess and what they do with it.

Some have shed loads of dosh but give generous donations to charities or to help others they know – and fair play to them. But others selfishly hoard all they own.

At the end of the day, laws should be in place to ensure that no-one has obscene amounts of wealth while others have nothing. That's morally indefensible.

There could still be plenty of scope for various levels of affluence in society without permitting such outrageous extremes.

So a certain degree of control would be needed to ensure they don't happen – another reason I'm not an anarchist.

March 10 – Well, the blood pressure gizmo's off and I'm back to normal – or at least my version of normal. When the device came off and the clinic nurse did a computer print-out from it, she said my BP levels were fine.

Now I have to book my annual blood test at my GP's surgery and make an appointment to see Dr Mitchell to discuss the results of that and the BP monitor readings.

Sunshine and Ice Volume Five, A Twist of Fate, has been out a year today – and late yesterday I took delivery of a box containing paperback versions of the newest published instalment, *Volume Eight, Patience and Wisdom*.

I'm going to hand out or post most of the copies to friends in the next few days and hold on to some books I'll give to family when I next see them.

So Volumes One to Eight will all be available in paperback form and on Kindle within the next couple of weeks or so.

And last week I made the final amendments to proofs of *Volume Nine, Diamonds and Gold*, so that should be out soon too. Fabulous!

Thank goodness for Author Essentials, my new publishers who rescued my books for a very reasonable fee when Indepenpress went bust.

On that happy note, I think I'm going to bring this first part of *Sunshine and Ice Volume Ten, Glittering Stars*, to a close.

Part two will follow in the blink of an eye…

****

GLITTERING STARS

Part Two

(March to May 2015)

CHAPTER SIX – EQUAL RIGHTS

March 11 – Today's a Wednesday and Sunday just gone (March 8) was International Women's Day – a time to honour females' rights and girl power in all its glorious forms. Quite right too – but why not do this all year round?

Some fellers might well have been thinking "what about us, why don't we have a special day?" And I must admit I had wondered, thinking surely sexual equality works both ways.

Well, apparently there already is such an event – a largely unmentioned and therefore unknown fact I discovered on checking with Google. International Men's Day is November 19 every year and it aims "to improve gender relations and promote unity."

So now we know.

A couple of hours ago I announced on Facebook the release of Patience and Wisdom – and it already has six "likes" – from my daughter-in-law Emily and my friends Theresa Bevis, Diana Slater, Steve Elvidge, Louise Davis and Victoria Brown. Nice!

March 12 – Carole Jones, Tina Wilkins, June Wade and Mark Hemington have also "liked" my status. Spread the word guys – and help to spread the love!

March 15 – It's Mother's Day so I'd like to wish all mums the very best. Hope each has a great time and is spoiled rotten!

It's also, of course, a poignant reminder of happier times to those of us whose parents have passed over. RIP Mum – and Dad – you're always in my heart.

Watching a programme on catch-up TV yesterday afternoon sent my mind spinning back to October 1979 and a rock concert I saw at Bournemouth Winter Gardens.

I was running the pop column in the *Times/Herald* series of local weekly newspapers, which entailed reviewing albums and attending gigs by visiting rock and pop acts.

I turned up at this one show by an up-and-coming group I didn't know anything about. I'd only heard their name. I hadn't heard any of their music.

But as I took my seat the air was crackling with a level of excitement I've rarely witnessed at a gig. And I've been to many over the years, some by total legends.

The support act, Tenpole Tudor, finished their set and the tension and anticipation built to fever pitch.

It was obvious the headliners were something special if they were able to generate this sort of a buzz before even hitting the stage.

And when they did, their electrifying set blew me away along with everyone else. They were just bloody amazing!

That was my introduction to the Undertones, one of Ireland's finest bands ever. I went out during my lunch break the following day and bought their first album on cassette.

Needless to say, I also wrote a glowing report for my pop column in the *Bournemouth Times* and its sister papers the *Christchurch Times*, *Swanage Times* and *Poole Herald*.

Feargal Sharkey and his band were just making a name for themselves and only had their debut album and a couple or three singles out at the time. I instantly became a fan and followed their career with great interest. But unfortunately that was the only time I saw them live.

I was reminded of that outstanding gig as I viewed the TV programme, a documentary telling the story of Irish rock music from Van Morrison and Them to current sensation the Strypes.

Along the way we were treated to fine music and wonderful memories courtesy of Thin Lizzy, Rory Gallagher, the Boomtown Rats, U2, the Undertones and Sinead O'Connor.

Sadly, I never saw U2 or Sinead, but I did catch both Lizzy and Rory twice, once at Reading Festival then again locally. I saw the Rats once at Poole. All were excellent.

I've just finished listening to a Jimi Hendrix compilation album and I'm going to sign off now and have some lunch. I decided on Jimi rather than any of the above having watched my DVD of the Hendrix story again last night. What a genius!

Oh I do love my music! Have I mentioned? – Ha ha!

March 17 – I've lit a candle in memory and honour of my treasured friend Pat Jones, whose birthday is today. Pat – Tom and Carole Jones' mum – is sadly no longer with us in this plane of existence.

But she lives on in our hearts – a funny, wise, lovely lady – my Pisces pal. RIP Pat.

Which means it's also Saint Patrick's Day – the Irish patron saint she was named after thanks to the timing of her birth.

I'm playing all Irish music to mark the event – a bit of Rory Gallagher, a bit of Undertones and, at the moment, a bit of U2.

Continuing the theme, Sam's invited me to hers later to have a few Paddy's day drinks and Carl and I are due to see the Black Star Riders – featuring former members of legendary Irish band Thin Lizzy – tomorrow night at Boscombe's O2 Academy.

It will be the second time I've seen the Riders. We attended their gig at the same venue in November 2013 and they were simply superb.

This time they're appearing in a doubler-header concert with Europe. I know, I know – before you say it, yes the group responsible for that dreadful chart-topping song The Final Countdown.

But that was a pop-tinged sell-out track designed to win mainstream recognition – with outstanding success (number one in 25 territories including the UK) – and they are in actual fact a mighty fine heavy rock band. Honest!

Turning to the news, a seventh UK healthcare worker has been flown home after suspected contact with Ebola – the highly infectious and potentially lethal virus that broke out in Africa in December 2013 and has so far killed more than 8,000 people.

The person, not yet named, worked in the same facility in Sierra Leone as a US volunteer medic who recently caught it.

The UK patient currently has no symptoms. They've been assessed and discharged from the Royal Victoria Infirmary in Newcastle. Officials assure they will be kept under close observation.

This is obviously a cause for great concern. There's no known cure for the virus at present and the mortality rate is very high. All medics can hope to do is identify and treat it quickly before it takes hold.

But there is good news. UK nurse Pauline Cafferkey, the first UK victim of the latest Ebola outbreak, has reportedly made a full recovery and is now out of hospital after returning from Sierra Leone with it in December.

Pauline was the second Briton to recover from the virus during the current crisis.

March 19 – Last night's gig was awesome. The Black Star Riders were just as excellent as the last time we saw them a year and a bit ago, and Joey Tempest and his band were just plain outstanding.

Loud and fast rock and roll, skilfully delivered and tight as a duck's arse. Even The Final Countdown sounded good, miles better live than on the record.

An added bonus was that we saw two these great rock acts for the price of one. It was a magnificent gig, but probably the last one I'll go to for a while now I'm pulling in my horns on the financial front.

But I'm not the only one. Chancellor George Osborne presented his last budget plans before the general election to the Commons yesterday, including his proposal to cut another £25 billion, half of it from the already badly-battered welfare fund.

This is despicable, but at least he's being honest, unlike Cameron, whose sickening attempts to sweet-talk voters apparently know no bounds.

And so the baby-kissing and question-swerving will no doubt continue in earnest until polling day, Thursday, May 7. Ye gods!

In other news, a Briton named as Sally Jane Adey was among more than 20 people shot dead at a museum in Tunis, Tunisia yesterday. Security forces killed two gunmen but are still searching for accomplices.

March 20 – It's 10am and I've just been to my local surgery for a routine blood test – an annual feature nowadays by order of Dr Mitchell. I get the results next week.

While I was there, we had a partial eclipse of the sun by the moon and I'm now watching TV pictures of the event.

It was too cloudy to see it round these parts on my way to and from the surgery but it did turn a shade darker and chillier and became eerily quiet.

Today's eclipse coincides with two other celestial features – a supermoon and the spring equinox.

A supermoon, or perigee moon, happens when the full or new moon passes closest to the Earth, making it look bigger than it usually does.

An equinox is the time of year when day and night are of equal duration, mid-way between the longest and shortest days. So we have two every year, the autumn equinox occurring in September.

The longest day is in June and the shortest, in December. All four are sacred to followers of the Earth religions and each marks the official start of a season, in today's case spring.

March 25 – Investigations are continuing after a plane carrying 150 people crashed in the French Alps yesterday.

The Germanwings Airbus A320 was on its way from Barcelona to Düsseldorf when the as-yet unexplained disaster occurred. It is believed no-one on board survived.

France, Germany and Spain are in mourning and the tragedy has sent shock waves across the world. Our thoughts are with the families of the passengers and crew.

****

CHAPTER SEVEN – TWISTED AGENDAS

March 26 – Right – let's get one thing straight here. I'm no apologist for nasty individuals with sick and twisted agendas inflicting mental torture, physical injury or worse on others. Readers of my books thus far might have concluded that I am.

So, to clarify – I do not condone wrongdoing in any way, shape or form and I despise the actions of those who ruthlessly and viciously exploit, terrorize or kill others.

But it becomes a different debate if misguided loyalty, muddled ideas of morality or confused thinking of any kind are involved.

An act of passion in the heat of the moment might also be understandable, especially if it's designed to avenge another's pain or protect them from further harm. Still very wrong, but understandable.

And it's in these less defined areas that lawyers can argue the rights and wrongs, the impacts and state-imposed penalties. They can also do so, in a limited way, in more clear-cut cases of premeditated, cold-blooded and brutal acts of violence and cruelty.

Yep – we're back to one of my favourite mantras – each case on its merits.

If opposing capital punishment makes me soft on crime, so be it. Such extreme forms of enforcing "justice" most certainly are pre-meditated, cold-blooded and brutal in my view. They're barbaric and just as evil as the original offence – maybe more so.

As for being a deterrent, no-one who lashes out in the heat of the moment with dire consequences is likely stop and think about their eventual punishment.

Taking any human life is wrong – regardless of circumstances. But if the person concerned has pleaded for it as a release from torment, again, it's understandable.

Regardless of the nature of the wrongdoing, we should try to pinpoint, comprehend and address the root cause in a bid to prevent future repetitions.

And speaking of repetitions, I'm probably echoing some of my earlier comments here, but I feel it's necessary in order to hopefully avoid any misunderstanding.

I guess what I've been saying all along is it's so easy to lob insults at people who have perceivably done wrong and demand they be severely dealt with.

Yet we're never as bold or vociferous when it comes to our own slip-ups. We choose to conveniently ignore them even though they might be as serious or even worse.

And locking away wrongdoers never solves the problems unless the reasons behind their actions are recognized and dealt with.

I've just had a facetious thought. I've been speaking of people's wrongdoing and my opening paragraph of this chapter referred to "nasty individuals with sick and twisted agendas." Hey, I've just realized – the general election's six weeks today!

March 27 – Went to see my GP, Dr Tim Mitchell, this morning to discuss the results of my recent annual blood test and the computer print-out from my yearly close encounter with a 24-hour BP monitor.

Basically, nothing's changed all that much – certainly not for the worst. My liver, kidneys and blood-sugar ratio all appear to be okay, my cholesterol level's fine and the BP graph once again encouraging.

I'm at slightly greater risk of a having a heart attack or stroke than I was a year ago. But Dr Mitchell said this was to be expected with the ageing process. He was generally pleased with the test results and I was naturally very relieved.

March 28 – It's now transpired that the Germanwings air crash the other day was caused deliberately by a suicidal pilot wanting to end it all.

I find it tragic that Andreas Lubitz had lost all faith in his own life – but to totally disregard the lives of everyone else on board was nothing short of criminal.

March 29 – Apparently Mr Lubitz had mental problems. We can sympathize but we still can't condone the taking of 150 other lives. And this new revelation does beg the question – why the deuce was he allowed to fly a plane full of passengers?

But on to lighter matters. Today's a Sunday and I had another fine evening in the Bell last night with mates including Mark Hemington, Clare Hayes, John Gaynor, John Palmer, Billy Clarkson, Jem Hannen and a guy called Jim (don't know his surname).

Guv'nors Laura and Mark circulated among their customers as rock covers band Beyond Redemption played songs by the likes of Thin Lizzy, UFO, Led Zeppelin, Bad Company, the Animals and the Cult. Super!

Friday I went to Sam and Carl's for a couple or three hours with them, Sharon Pendleton, Becca, Albert the dog and Sam's cousin Diane.

What with the very satisfactory surgery visit on Friday morning, it's been a good weekend all round for yours truly.

Another result in the last few days has been a change in my television viewing arrangements with Virgin Media. I've shaved £20 off my monthly bills for telly, broadband internet access and a phone landline by dropping a few TV channels.

Not only that, my new Tivo box, replacing my old V-Plus model, is far better and I get a clearer picture. And once again the system's linked to my DVD/CD player and feeds through two stereo speakers donated by Jem a few years ago, so I get great sound quality too whether I'm watching TV or a DVD or playing music.

Speaking of which, I'm listening to a CD as I type. It features a reggae-style rendition of Pink Floyd's Dark Side of the Moon album by the Easy Star All Stars. Brilliant!

I've also got their version of the Beatles' classic LP Sergeant Pepper, which isn't as good as it doesn't seem to lend itself quite so well to such an arrangement.

March 31 – Well, the political campaigns are in full swing now with five weeks to go to the general election. Devious, deluded and deranged politicians are hoping we're all dim, gullible and very, very forgetful when it comes to the damage they've caused.

And this applies to Conservative, Labour and Liberal Democrat parties in equal measure.

It's a sickening sight – smooth-talking dream weavers sucking up to voters with outlandish promises to benefit us all while stubbornly refusing to define exactly how when pressed for inconvenient details.

Take our glorious Prime Minister, for example. David Cameron was on the TV news this morning pledging to create two million more jobs if he gets back into Downing Street. But he won't say what sort of jobs or where – now there's a surprise!

One thing's for sure – they won't be real, reliable or lasting sources of the vital funds people need to pay their bills. Not proper jobs as most of us would interpret the term.

No, they'll involve notoriously unreliable zero hours contracts, part-time or temporary posts or unpaid work that gets people off the dole in the short term only.

And besides, how the heck does the PM's rash pronouncement square with warnings of £25 billion more government spending cutbacks if he and his lot are re-elected?

What a gross insult to our intelligence!

It's been independently estimated that more than a million extra people would be thrown out of work if such savage measures were implemented.

So much for Cameron's ridiculous assertions that the economy he's wrecked is recovering and we're heading towards full employment. The man's living in cloud cuckoo land!

Not only that, he has the brass neck to claim that standards of living are improving. Not in my neighbourhood, pal!

Seems to me the terms "homeless", "food bank", "credit crisis", "company closures", "job losses", "rent arrears" and "repossession" aren't in this guy's vocabulary.

And yet, strangely, "budget cuts" is – unless he's outrageously promising mass job creation. Begs the question – can't he see the connections between his own policies and the sorry state of our battered, beleaguered and demoralised country?

Well, of course he can, but he doesn't care. He's blithe arrogance personified. Oh how I dearly wish he comes seriously unstuck on May 7 and loses his stranglehold grip on our poor nation.

I also hope Clegg and his cronies also suffer big time for their unforgivable treachery.

But I also find Labour's bold promises more than a bit rich, bearing in mind their own dismal record in government in the Blair and Brown years – especially the wars, their tendency to favour money men over everyone else and their own welfare budget cuts.

What with UKIP, the Greens and the Scottish National Party also in the mix, it's going to be a very close-run thing this time around and the outcome is difficult to call.

And, just two days into the campaigning period proper, I'm already sick to the back teeth of all the lies and bull crap and yearning for it all to be over. Roll on May 8!

Actually, thinking about it, that's when the real fun and games could start if there's no overall winner and frantic deal brokering ensues as the parties bid to seize power.

Asked about such a scenario, Green leader Natalie Bennett today categorically ruled out any kind of alliance with the Tories. And that's music to my ears.

April 1 – Our individual pasts can't be changed but we should work together to improve our shared future – for all our sakes.

April 2 – It's so nice to run into an old mate you haven't seen for ages and stop for a brief catch-up chat, isn't it?

This happened to me the other day when I was shopping in Boscombe and met Alan Painter, one of my Bell drinking buddies back in the day when his nickname was Kwik Fit Al.

He was working for the local branch of the famous MOT testing and car parts firm at the time and besides, the moniker helped distinguish him from other Bell/White Horse regulars also called Alan.

He and his lady, Debi Browning, are Facebook friends of mine, as is Debi's sister Beccy, a Bell barmaid.

Al supports Bournemouth and Liverpool football clubs and, by a strange quirk of fate, a few seconds after leaving him I encountered another old Bell/Horse face I hadn't seen for yonks called Everton Tony, a proud Liverpudlian who supports the rival club.

By the way, *Sunshine and Ice Volume Nine: Diamonds and Gold* is now out.

The cover is the best of all my books so far with its attractive gold and light blue colour scheme – or at least it would be except for one unfortunate and prominent error on the first few paperback copies printed.

The rest of the book is fine but the front bears the words *"Sunshine and Ice Volume Eight: Patience and Wisdom"*, repeating the title of my previous instalment. I've told my publishers so hopefully this will be corrected for future copies.

April 2, later – John Lennon's first wife, Cynthia, has died at her home in Spain, aged 75. The cause was cancer, according to a piece on their son Julian's website.

The couple started a relationship after meeting as fellow students at art school when John, Paul McCartney and George Harrison were just making their first forays into the music world and pop stardom was still a dream.

Cynthia became pregnant so John decided to do the right thing and marry her – just as the Beatles started their meteoric rise to the top. Manager Brian Epstein insisted it be kept secret as he wanted all his boys to appear available to teenaged girl fans.

But the rumours quickly started to circulate and the fact was confirmed a year and a bit later on the band's triumphant first American tour.

The couple had a tough time as the pressures of global fame took their toll and they split in 1968. Cynthia married three more times but admits in her two autographical books that although he treated her badly the rock star was the love of her life.

Sir Paul McCartney said he was very sad at the news of Cynthia's passing. He had great memories of his times with a "lovely lady" who was a good mother to Julian. Ringo Starr and Lennon's second wife Yoko Ono also paid tributes.

With nothing much on telly last night, I decided to watch again my DVD of Stanley Kubrick's classic film *A Clockwork Orange*. I'd forgotten how good it was.

This movie is a masterpiece – Kubrick's treatment of Anthony Burgess's brilliant book and his use of diverse music and shocking imagery is dazzling and inspired.

It's powerful, unsettling and remains controversial – and it's amazing to think how bold it was for 1971, the year it was released, caused an outrage and got banned.

The film poses the extremely awkward and uncomfortable question – are sick and twisted thugs who brutally assault others and use rape and murder to get their kicks actually the inevitable by-products of a brutal, sick and twisted society?

Mad scientists, sadistic prison warders, violent policemen, creepy probation officers, aggressive tramps and callous, seedy politicians also feature in a mesmerising movie.

And I can't listen to excerpts from Beethoven's Ninth Symphony or Gene Kelly's Singing in the Rain without immediately thinking of this film.

I had to check and, oh dear – yes I had incredibly and unforgivably forgotten *A Clockwork Orange* when listing my preferences in Persistent Illusions.

I had also omitted the Breakfast Club – another film I never tire of. A great script and superb acting turn the seemingly unimpressive and quite dull plot about five high school kids in detention into a wonderful study of human attitudes and behaviour.

April 3 – It's Good Friday, a sombre and sacred time for Christians – the day they mark the barbaric execution of their religion's founder.

Y'shua bar Yosef, better known to the modern world as Jesus Christ, was nailed to a wooden cross – some versions of the story say a tree – and suffered an excruciating death by crucifixion because he was said to be a dangerous religious and political subversive liable to spark a bloody revolution.

Any follower of the Christian faith will tell you that the authorities had seriously misunderstood his altruistic intentions and his willing submission to this gruesome fate was the ultimate sacrifice to appease God for all humanity's sins.

They will also say that the story has a happy ending because he was later restored to life and then became a holy spirit residing in Heaven for eternity at God's right hand.

And they'll assert that anyone who believes this, repents their wrongdoings and does good for others will join the deity and their ascended leader in everlasting bliss.

In contrast, those who persist in bad behaviour will burn in Hell's fires, they claim.

My take on all this is detailed in my earlier books. Briefly, I tend to accept that that he was a real person preaching peace, harmony and helping others. He was imbued with divinity – a driving force for good and a potent emblem of the positive energy stream.

The core message of the gospels is one of sound values and decent living that no-one could reasonably argue with.

As for all the other stuff that's overlaid the religion, I'm not so sure. I think the virgin birth and resurrection accounts are vivid symbolism, not to be taken too literally.

There's great truth and wisdom in the New Testament and many parts of the Old, and also in most other spiritual books. They can be employed to greatly improve lives.

And at the end of the day, if people with unshakable faith in any religious texts are inspired to spread love, peace and harmony, that's great, isn't it? Good on 'em, I say.

It becomes a whole different ball game when they twist their understanding of the sayings and stories in a bid to justify division, pain and murder. That's just plain evil.

Changing the subject, last night was an historic one as we watched the first ever live televised election debate involving seven UK political leaders.

Tory leader David Cameron, our Prime Minister for the past five years, faced his own Liberal Democrat sidekick Nick Clegg, Labour's Ed Miliband and four others in a fascinating verbal tussle before a live studio audience and seven million viewers.

The other leaders were Nigel Farage of the UKIP, the Greens' Natalie Bennett, Nicola Sturgeon of the Scottish National Party and Leanne Wood of the Welsh Plaid Cymru.

For my money, the three women came out best, challenging austerity with voices of reason, humanity and common decency that truly represented the people.

Farage came across as a foreigner-hating buffoon and Cameron as a smug, arrogant man constantly blowing his own trumpet.

He and Miliband seemed more interested in firing cheap shots at each other than answering any of the questions put forward by audience members.

Both quoted figures a lot but in a very unconvincing way.

Nick Clegg was making similar points to those he had prior to the last election – that is, before he attained power and was unmasked as a weak and traitorous turncoat.

And it was nauseating watching him and Cameron swapping insults after five years of working hand-in-glove to jointly run our poor country into the ground.

The questions raised centred on immigration, the National Health Service and planned future cuts in government spending.

Did the answers help floating voters make up their minds? In the case of the smaller parties, quite possibly. As for the so-called big three, who knows? – I doubt it.

Because that was the big difference in my view – the SNP, Plaid Cymru, UKIP and Green leaders each represented a fresh new approach, while the Tory, Labour and Lib Dem men proposed more of the same old, same old that's been the UK's ruin.

April 4 – What with it being Easter weekend and all, I've been thinking more about Christian beliefs – and particularly the strange, disturbing notions of Heaven and Hell.

Some are scared stiff of burning in Satan's fiery pit if they don't live virtuous lives. Others tie themselves in knots trying to grasp and explain such metaphysical ideas.

But, as with the virgin birth and returning from the dead, I feel deep symbolism has been taken at face value as material fact.

The way I see it, Heaven could well be code for the afterlife and Hell a metaphor for the misery and ugliness in our physical plane of existence

With regard to all the "sinners will burn for eternity" talk – Well, that hardly squares with my vision of a nurturing force for good and my dearly-held desire and belief that love, peace and unity will always win in the end over hatred, hostility and division.

But frightened people are so much easier to control.

God is often spoken of as a father figure. The Lord's Prayer, a cornerstone of Christianity, even starts with the words "Our Father, who art in Heaven."

So I ask – why oh why would a loving parent allow any of their offspring to suffer so terribly? Or threaten them with such a horrendous fate? Clerics struggle with that one.

As I've said many times, I could be wrong – very wrong. And I reserve the right to change my mind at any time if new information and ideas come to light.

Unlike others, I don't claim to have all the answers – far from it. These are very complex issues that theologists with degrees have difficulty understanding.

All any of us can do is formulate our beliefs and opinions based on how we feel about what we've been told. Gut instinct can be invaluable here – just so long as we're attuned to our own higher selves.

April 5 – Happy Easter folks. Yes, it's Easter Sunday and so far I've had a good one. Yesterday I went to Sam and Carl's for an egg-hunt party for the kids followed by a booze and fun session for the adults when the little ones went to bed or went home.

Well, I say adults but when you're talking about us lot it's a pretty flexible term. Apart from Sam, Carl and me, Kelly Adams was there along with Sam's cousins Diane and Laura, Jem Hannen and Sam's grown-up daughter Bec.

Tina Mcauley attended for a short while in the afternoon and a chap called Jimmy turned up later to collect his daughter Molly.

The other children included Sam and Carl's two boys Rudy and Bailey plus Storm, Hudson and Pacey, Kelly's three kids. And a good time was had by all.

The only sour note came when I got a take-away, went home and opened a kitchen cupboard to get a plate. I accidentally bashed myself in the mouth, knocking loose a tooth.

So loose, in fact, that when I started to eat my fish and chips it came out completely. That means I've now lost both my large front teeth, the other being a casualty of the assault I suffered at Christmas 2001.

I'll have to get a second false tooth put on the denture I wear when I'm out.

Speaking of notes, I've been listening to a right old hotchpotch of music over the weekend. A bit of Lou Reed, a smattering of

Europe, a Bob Seger album, Jean Michel Jarre, Jimi Hendrix, Mike Oldfield and the Ozric Tentacles.

The who whats? I must admit I'd never heard of that last band either until Carl recommended them to me. They're trancey, spacey, eclectic and quite out there – the kind of group you either love or hate.

If you like Hawkwind, Leftfield, Tangerine Dream, Dreadzone and Kraftwerk, as I do, I think you'd find them both interesting and appealing. Great music for chilling.

On the telly front, ITV Three has been showing back to back Carry On films – great fun! Okay, they're a bit dated and display cringe-worthy attitudes in places, but they're still highly entertaining with fabulous comic timing and clever wordplay.

April 7, 10pm – Sam and Carl had an impromptu barbeque today as the weather was so nice and sunny. Along with them, myself, Rudy and Bailey, others taking part were Kelly Adams, Hudson, a friend called Kathy, her daughter Grace, Bec, Ryan Millen and Albert the dog. Sweet!

April 8, 6pm – My doorbell rang this afternoon and, answering it, I found a delivery guy carrying a cardboard box he wanted me to sign for, which I duly did.

Returning to my flat, I opened the box to find several crisp fresh paperback copies of *Sunshine and Ice Volume Nine: Diamonds and Gold* – this lot with the right title on the front cover.

They really are impressive – the best-looking of all the volumes published so far. Well done, Author Essentials – and thanks for the new batch, which I hadn't expected.

Such a shame I've already mailed or handed out most of the books from the previous boxful that was delivered to me, bearing the wrong wording on the front.

Oh well – if my writings make me famous, these paperbacks might be worth good money, like misprinted postage stamps that fetch small fortunes. We can all dream.

April 9 – Happy birthday Steve Mitchell, I wonder where you are now and what you're up to buddy.

Steve was the first friend I made at infants' school when we were both six years old. We grew up together but lost contact when he went abroad – Spain I think – and I moved from Slough to Dorset in the late 1970s.

Oh dear! – As the political arguments intensify in the run-up to May's election, it's got all ugly and personal over the thorny issue of our nuclear defence policy.

Basically, Labour wants to retain our Trident missile system and the Conservatives are keen to upgrade it. The Scottish National Party, the Welsh Plaid Cymru and the Greens propose it be scrapped altogether.

With the two main parties neck-and-neck, many voters still undecided and the poll's eventual outcome anyone's guess, the prospect of another coalition government is looming large.

SNP leader Nicola Sturgeon has stated categorically that her party would never strike a deal with the Tories but would do so with Labour if it kept the blue rosette brigade from returning to Downing Street.

And she turned the screw last night by saying the Trident issue was non-negotiable.

This has spurred defence secretary Michael Fallon to warn this morning that Labour would cave in to the SNP's demands if it meant seizing power.

We'd thus be left defenceless at a time outside threats were growing, he claimed.

And he launched a personal attack on Ed Miliband, saying he'd stabbed his own brother in the back to get Labour's top job and now he was thinking of doing the same to the nation over Trident.

Miliband has so far declined to retaliate, saying he can take personal insults like this on the chin. But he firmly denied he would gamble with our defences as alleged.

My view of all this is that Michael Fallon's rash and irresponsible comments show just how worried, panicked and desperate to win the Conservatives are getting as the election approaches.

I'm not sure why, because I'd say they're doing surprisingly well considering the devastation they've caused across our country over the past five years.

Ironically, the defence secretary's scaremongering and personal attack could actually backfire and lose votes for the Tories – not a bad thing, thinking about it.

But such unwarranted insults should have no place in electioneering. I say state your policies clearly, answer questions honestly and directly and leave it up to voters to decide who has the best arguments. And that applies to all of them, not just him.

As for Fallon's alarmist claim that outside threats are growing, I'd suggest a good way to halt this would be to stop picking fights on foreign soil that increase the danger of attacks on us here at home in the UK.

Oh and how the freaking hell can we afford Trident anyway if we're still belt-tightening and more cuts are on the way? So much for the need for austerity!

A single Trident missile costs £16 million and it's estimated that the bill for updating the whole system, as Cameron and crew want, could be more than £30 billion.

How can they possibly reconcile this extravagance with their budget pruning that continues to cause such widespread misery across our battered and beloved nation?

Fallon's hawkish stance and ridiculous assertion that Labour would leave us wide open to attack should be treated with the utter contempt they deserve.

This sort of bolshie talk, linked to aggressive foreign policies, only raises the stakes for all of us. If you want to save yourself from attack don't give others reason to.

Okay, fair enough, there are occasions when nasty aggressors genuinely threaten or actually inflict injury or worse on groupings or individuals. I know this all too well.

But at the national level, I'd say keep a strong defence network in place but never use it to strike first or to take military action abroad unless it's absolutely the last resort.

And if we can't afford to pay people much-needed benefits and provide them with essential domestic front-line services (a massive if by the way – my deep scepticism is well documented) we certainly can't afford overblown defence budgets either.

But there I go again, being naïve. Battle hardware can be very lucrative indeed and money heads lacking morals are able to cash in big time by selling expensive weapons and also by rebuilding the infrastructures of nations ravaged by war.

And this occurs regardless of which of the two big parties is in power. Suspicion, paranoia, splits and conflict are great for business, very welcome news for some.

April 10 – The cricket world is mourning the death of legendary Australian player and commentator Richie Benaud, aged 84.

He played in 63 Tests, 28 as captain, before retiring in 1964 to pursue a career in journalism and broadcasting.

He subsequently became the highly-recognizable voice of cricket all over the globe His final commentary in England came during the 2005 Ashes series but he continued to work for Channel Nine in his home country until 2013.

Last November, he revealed that he was being treated for skin cancer. Now he's gone. Flags are at half mast and tributes have poured in.

Meanwhile, in Kenya, the government is trying to restore public confidence in its security forces a week after 148 people were killed, apparently by Islamic militants, at a college in the north of the country.

So, once again, ethnic conflict seems to have led to the multiple deaths of innocent people. Ye Gods! – And I use that expression deliberately in this context, for whichever deity you believe in, this is shocking, very wrong and so, so tragic.

It's also bitterly ironic if radical Muslims were actually involved as alleged – because it makes this yet another case of homicidal crazies using religion as an excuse for mass murder. When oh when will it end?

It makes me both sad and angry – but before anyone calls for a violent reaction, I would warn that this would just make things worse, piling misery on misery.

As Gandhi once wisely said, an eye for an eye makes the whole world blind.

****

CHAPTER EIGHT – BROKEN PROMISES

April 11 – I try really hard to ignore the politicians' outrageous and implausible promises as they try to win votes in the run-up to an election.

It's amazing what unbelievable nonsense these shameless people spout in their desperate bids to sweet-talk the people.

As a rule I give them all a wide berth and resist the urge to get drawn into the arguments – but I just couldn't let this little gem go without comment.

Today's TV news informed us that Crapmeister Cameron had pledged to spend an extra £8 billion a year on the NHS by 2020 if his party was returned to power.

Yes, he really, really said that, apparently. What utter bilge water!

This is the same guy who a few months ago oversaw the disgraceful refusal of a one per cent pay rise for health staff amid wild claims it would throw 15,000 nurses out of work – just as MPs were preparing to grant themselves a 10 per cent salary increase!

He's also the man who's been at the helm of a government that's pruned essential services to the bone and withdrawn vital welfare payments from the ill and disabled with serious, sometimes fatal, consequences.

Whose cruel and callous mantra has been "cuts, cuts and more cuts" as his mad austerity measures have caused widespread devastation, traumatising the populace.

He's even warned that another £25 billion worth of cuts are on the way if his party returns to power.

And now he expects us to believe he's willing to inject billions more into our health service! Where on Earth's that money coming from if the coffers are as empty as he's constantly claimed in his vain attempts to justify these swingeing cutbacks?

Or, to put it another way, just how gullible does he think we are? How dare he insult our intelligence so blatantly!

Incredibly, some folk will actually buy this garbage while others are so terrified of Labour getting in they'll actually vote for this despicable Tory crew that's spent five years grinding our nation into the dust, destroying morale and causing untold misery.

Seems to me some people just don't care what big fat fibs they need to tell in their desperation to win favour and persuade us to overlook the pain they've inflicted.

Labour and the Lib Dems are just as bad. They've all made numerous pledges in their election speeches only to backtrack on them when actually getting into government.

The usual excuses are "we didn't realise things were that bad," or "we didn't foresee such and such." Pathetic! – don't make assurances you're not certain you can keep!

Okay, granted, some events are unexpected and politicians as a rule can't gaze into the future. But most of the time their broken promises centre on matters they should have been aware of or anticipated.

Good grief! – They're supposed to have skilled, alert experts advising them!

And before some bright spark suggests that the extra NHS money could come from savings made on the welfare budget, I'd make the following points:

Firstly, health services and benefit payments should both be very high up on any decent, civilised government's spending agenda and it should never be a question of either/or – especially when huge savings could be made elsewhere (HS2, Trident and a whole plethora of non-essential items).

Secondly, as far as I know Cameron and crew have never said they're pruning some budgets in order to boost others – or at least not all that loudly. They've always screamed that Labour left the nation broke in trying to justify their savage cutbacks.

Thirdly, if they can afford to spend billions more on the NHS, surely a small portion of that could be used to award workers in that sector a reasonable pay increase?

And fourthly, don't you find it interesting that this unexpected and unconvincing new promise of extra health services funding comes after the dissolution of Parliament pending the election in just 26 days' time? Who's he trying to kid?

April 13 – Readers of my books thus far might well have concluded – quite wrongly – that as an avid pacifist I have a problem with soldiers. Not true – not true at all!

I have the utmost respect for all our armed forces and the poor souls killed in action or returning from duty physically or mentally devastated. That's why I firmly support Help for Heroes, Homes for Heroes, the Royal British Legion and so on.

My beef is with the politicians who send these decent, patriotic individuals into unnecessary and tragically lethal battles in far-flung territories on foreign soil.

For goodness' sake, these people are supposed to be defending us from harm, not partaking in imperialistic, ideological battles thousand of miles away. That sucks!

The clue's in the description morons! It's called defence for a very good reason – attacking others abroad for dubious motives should never be part of the plan.

Yes I'm a pacifist. But I firmly believe in defence, real defence – a strong military presence to protect us from aggressors posing a genuine threat to our country.

Bless you, service personnel. Screw you, war-mongering politicians! Why don't you go to the front line yourselves and do your own dirty work? I can see the excuses coming thick and fast. Horrible gits!

April 14 – Yesterday was a very enjoyable one. Sam's son Alex, these days living and working as a chef in Wiltshire, was visiting so she and Carl organised a barbeque.

Apart from those three and me, Alex's sister Becca was there plus Sam and Carl's two little boys Rudy and Bailey, Kelly Adams, her young lad Hudson, Sam's cousin Laura and her little son, and Ryan Millen.

Becca's terrier dog Albert and other pets were also in evidence and our mate Jem Hannen came along later. It was a jolly good burger, booze and fun session.

April 15 – The Green Party yesterday launched its election manifesto, reflecting pretty accurately my own views and values as previously outlined.

In a nutshell, we promote a fairer, more truly democratic, environment-protecting, compassionate society where the disadvantaged are helped not hindered and it's not all about hard cash and stark statistics.

But there's one policy that might appear at first glance to conflict with some of my earlier comments – and that concerns immigration, or more accurately, migration.

The party backs the free movement of labour across European borders. I do too – in principle. My concern arises over the sheer volumes of people coming to our shores. I think these should be better controlled and managed.

Totals should be kept to reasonable limits and there should be much less of a heavy bias towards Europeans and a lot more parity between these nationalities and others from the old Commonwealth countries and elsewhere.

And it goes without saying that we should be carefully guarded against the import of fatal diseases and terrorism.

Of course, these are the sort of things UKIP leader Nigel Farage would say – but there's a striking difference in our reasons for saying them.

I'm neither a racist nor a bigot, and I would argue that this is all common sense for a small island like ours with finite resources.

I also advocate strongly that immigration rules are exercised using compassion and fairness rather than inflexible box-ticking and iron-fist enforcement of crude formulas and ice-cold numbers.

But Farage's alarmingly right-wing party seems to attract racists and bigots with frightening regularity and he himself seems to constantly blame immigrants for most of our country's problems.

Whichever issue's under discussion in the run-up to the election, he bangs on about them like a cracked record. It's getting really boring.

April 17 – As if to prove the point, Farage was in typically blunt and offensive form during a second live televised debate last night, this time on the BBC.

Rival company ITV's historic programme a fortnight ago was the first ever live show featuring seven political leaders sharing a stage to discuss questions raised by a studio audience.

But, amazingly, Tory Prime Minister David Cameron and his Lib-Dem deputy Nick Clegg, both present for the first debate, were both conspicuously absent last night.

The other five leaders from the first show were back for more – namely, foreigner-baiting Farage, Labour's Ed Miliband, Nicola Sturgeon of the Scottish National Party, Leanne Wood of the Welsh Plaid Cymru and the Green Party's Natalie Bennett.

Once again, the three women really impressed and once again Farage ranted on about immigrants in answer to every question raised.

He was just plain obnoxious. Not content with insulting the other four, he even turned on the studio audience, with predictable results. What a detestable plonker!

His blinkered and nasty stance totally ignores the fact that on balance immigrants bring a heck of a lot more to our fair land than they take from it.

He also seems to miss the point that free movement of labour throughout Europe – subject to certain common-sense controls and limits – is very much a two-way thing, also benefiting people born here who want to live and work or claim welfare abroad.

How would any of us feel if we went to another country to be confronted by its version of him?

In Cameron's absence, Ed Miliband seized his chance to positively shine as a potential rival prime minister. His skilled performance no doubt won him many friends across the country.

His only mistake, I feel, came right at the end when he rejected outright Nicola Sturgeon's offer to work together to defeat the Tories. He could rue that rash reaction if he's later put in a position where he has no choice if he wants to seize power.

Especially when Leanne Wood and Natalie Bennett had also just said that they would never prop up a Conservative government but might be willing to co-operate with Labour – up to a point – if it kept the Tories out of Downing Street.

This was a green light for Miliband. Of course he wants to win outright, but if he doesn't and still has the chance to be Prime Minister of a Labour-led government, why oh why didn't he leave the door open? He was doing so well up to that point!

Farage, by contrast, was very much the odd one out, ostracized, isolated and alone. Serves him right for being such a humourless, odious dolt!

As for Cameron and Clegg – why on Earth did they swerve last night's debate? Was it cowardice or arrogance? Either way, it could cost them dearly – Cameron might have blown any chance of winning the election and Clegg of regaining any credibility.

Oh, and the monthly unemployment figures came out today, showing another drop – yeah right! The 19th-century Conservative Prime Minister Benjamin Disraeli is often credited with coining the phrase "there are lies, damned lies and statistics." Quite!

Lifting the mood somewhat, today's my Auntie Joyce's birthday. I rang her a bit earlier to wish her all the best and we had a chat.

April 19 – How mad and tragic it is that it takes the feared deaths of hundreds at sea to prise the media away from its tediously incessant coverage of the election build-up.

The news was broken earlier today that a boat carrying up to 700 migrants had capsized in the Mediterranean Sea.

The vessel, thought to be just 70 feet long, overturned just south of the Italian island of Lampedusa. So far only 28 people have been rescued and 24 bodies retrieved.

So for once the TV and newspaper journalists were forced to report on something else than the false promises of politicians trying to win votes in the crucial poll on May 7.

Well, I say journalists but these pathetically compliant media folk are acting more like the candidates' PR firms than impartial investigators trying to uncover the truth.

I mean, take just two examples – the monthly jobless figures mentioned above and the so-called deficit used as an excuse for damaging cruel and unfair austerity measures.

Both are usually taken at face value as indisputable fact without any attempts being made to probe, question and challenge in order to find out of this is actually the case.

I find this both worrying and depressing.

April 21 – Wishing a very happy fourth birthday to my grandson Lucas. Have a great time, precious boy.

Meanwhile, in world news, the Tunisian captain of the boat that capsized in the Mediterranean between Italy and Libya on Sunday, killing hundreds of migrants, has been charged with reckless multiple homicides, say Italian officials.

He's also accused, along with a crew member, with favouring illegal immigration.

Both were among 27 survivors who arrived in Sicily late on Monday.

I'm part-way through reading a fascinating book called *Your Life After Death*. Yeah, I know – sounds pretty morbid and scary. But it's not at all.

It's actually optimistic, joyous, encouraging and quite life-affirming.

It's written by a guy called Michael G Reccia, who purports to channel an ancient and highly-evolved spiritual entity called Joseph who gives an enlightening view of existence beyond the grave.

Joseph, via Michael, explains in easily understandable terms the complex and multi-faceted spiritual realms and the journey souls take when they leave our Earth plane.

I can hear the cynics and atheists already. Are you kidding Money? Don't tell us you're actually buying all this religious mumbo-jumbo!

Well, yes, I might be as it goes, for a lot of it accords with my own views developed over the years, and especially since my spiritual breakthrough, recorded in *A New Perspective*.

As always, I keep an open mind to all possibilities. But the way I see it, books like this ring a lot truer to me than the rigid, dogmatic, rather crude and all too simplistic notions of good and evil, Heaven and Hell embedded in the great faiths.

Indeed, Michael suggests that Joseph is speaking from a higher, more evolved, wiser and more enlightened viewpoint than those souls, steeped in religious indoctrination, that have passed over with lop-sided, flawed or incomplete ideas of the afterlife.

It's not all sweetness and light and there are unpleasant aspects. Souls journeying beyond the grave – and that means all souls, whether they believe in an afterlife or not – have to confront and deal with the pain and suffering they've caused in this reality.

They need to be reconciled with those they've hurt and make peace with them before continuing their spiritual journey.

Some souls feel the pull of the physical Earth plane so strongly they have a burning desire to return, possibly considering that they have unfinished business.

So they are reincarnated, in certain cases again and again, until they grasp that they don't have to and in fact their ultimate destiny is to break out of the cycle and avoid this happening, instead managing to progress to the next, higher spiritual level.

Just after death, many souls are confused, frightened and even angry, and that anger can rebound on them in a hurtful way.

Certain spiritual entities might even be tortured by visions of Hell – but these will be of their own making, part of a persistent illusion that's a construct of the imagination.

But, says Joseph, all this is temporary and eventually each soul reaches the higher spheres where light and love abound. So there's a happy ending for all of us, the only difference being some will experience it far sooner than others (as we view time).

That depends on how well we've grasped the profound, eternal truths involved here and responded to them, he says.

All this seems to me a far more sophisticated, subtle, complex, compassionate and refined version of ultra-realities and spiritual wisdom than those evoked by the vivid picture-language ideas so deeply ingrained in the world's major religions.

But such ideas are so powerful in some people that they can take a grip on their minds – the individual sparks of consciousness giving souls intelligence – so firm that they're carried with them from the physical plane into the spiritual life beyond.

Those sparks of consciousness are themselves part of the One God Consciousness – their original source and eventual home – even though many have forgotten.

Joseph says that this widespread, highly damaging amnesia came after a cataclysmic event aeons ago that he calls The Fall – seen in many religious schools as mankind's fall from grace with God, the subject of John Milton's epic poem *Paradise Lost*.

Such notions are often saturated in rich symbolism with colourful imagery conjuring up potent visions of Heaven and Hell, Satan and salvation.

But these, too, are rather basic and misleading versions of far subtler eternal truths that can also be carried into the spirit realms, says Joseph.

And his bottom line is the same as mine – when all's said and done, each of us is part of Oneness – God – and the sooner we realise this, the better. Our confusion, pain and anger all come from our self-imposed but erroneous concepts of isolation.

We wrongly believe we're physical entities trying to be spiritual but in fact we're spiritual entities struggling like mad in a flawed but dogged illusion of physicality.

And this illusion is often taken across the life-death threshold by the soul's consciousness, meaning that on first entering the spiritual realm the soul perceives it as being very similar to the physical one it's just left.

There can be landscapes, buildings and people– animals even – and the human-looking residents can initially appear to have bodies much the same as on Earth.

Newly-arrived souls can see themselves journeying by car, train or boat. They have the right idea, but the truth is much subtler than that.

It's only as the spiritual entity evolves and loses false perceptions of physicality and isolation that it sees more clearly the new situation it's now in – a mode of existence populated by beings emanating dazzling light, beautiful colour and harmonious sound.

Concepts such as ego, loneliness and division melt away in an atmosphere of peace and love, joy and unity. Sounds wonderful!

As I said, I'm only half-way through this book. But it gives me great comfort and hope. It has an air of authenticity, integrity and wisdom that strikes a chord in me.

By the way, I'm playing a Hawkwind album while typing this and my current computer desktop wallpaper (temporarily hidden as I write) is a photo of Egypt's Giza pyramids at dusk as the sun goes down. It all seems so appropriate somehow.

April 23 – Happy Saint George's Day everyone. Two weeks to go to the election.

And a mate of mine made a very interesting point the other day that's often largely overlooked in all the pre-poll razzmatazz.

He said, quite rightly, that general election voters were supposed to be choosing the person they thought would best represent their locality in Parliament.

They weren't voting for Cameron, or Miliband, or Clegg, unless they actually lived in the constituencies where these fellers were standing. But many people wrongly thought they were, he said.

True, but I think that's inevitable when candidates identify themselves so closely with national political parties in a poll affecting the whole of the UK. My friend is technically correct, but general elections have for ages been all about who governs us.

The more MPs that are elected wearing the same colour rosettes means the more seats that party has in the Commons – therefore a better chance of being put in charge of running the country. I'm not saying that's right or wrong – it's just the way it is.

My mate's comment actually becomes far more pertinent in the case of local council elections. But even then many candidates proudly represent the national political party backing and funding their campaign – unless they stand as an independent of course.

And I oppose tactical voting. Go the way your heart tells you to and have the courage of your own convictions. Otherwise, there's no hope at all of ever seeing the changes you probably yearn for.

People who bang on about the futility of so-called "wasted votes" are being depressingly defeatist in my view, playing right into the hands of our badly flawed system and the politicians who run it.

The same applies to those who choose not to vote. They have no right at all to criticize any government that gets into power then takes decisions they don't like.

April 24 – Sam and Carl invited me up to theirs for a few Saint George's Day drinkies yesterday. Super! – and the weather was fine so we were out in the garden until the children went to bed and it turned a bit chilly.

April 26 – Today's the day of the annual London Marathon at which thousands of people, many in fancy dress, raise loads of money for a variety of very worthy causes.

Good on 'em I say, but I won't be watching it on TV. Such events are fantastic communal gatherings and an excellent way of helping charities while keeping fit, but as a spectacle they just don't flick my switch. Sorry, but that's the way it is.

Touching on this subject again reminds me of something I said in an earlier book that might have been misconstrued by some readers.

I was writing about devious people defrauding the system by claiming sickness and disability benefits while running marathons or playing squash.

I sincerely hope no-one thought I was having a pop at the disabled. I would never do that. I wasn't talking about the genuinely disadvantaged, but the dishonest, able-bodied cheats doing paid work on the sly or having sufficient other funds to draw on.

Such greedy, self-centred scoundrels give all claimants a bad name.

I'm well aware that some participants in these races are blind or in wheelchairs or have other health issues. I have great admiration for their spirit and stubborn refusal to allow their handicaps or illnesses define them. The same applies to other sports.

And I would never begrudge such folk claiming any kind of welfare benefits should they feel the need to. They certainly shouldn't be hassled or pressurized in any way.

Some disabled people have paid work and others are keen to secure it. They should be positively encouraged in this – with the vital proviso that they feel up to it. Others have enough money to manage without any help from the state.

But disadvantaged folk without the financial safety nets of good incomes, substantial savings or other resources should be able to claim welfare without question – if, of course, they have authentic reasons and can satisfy set criteria.

Once again I stress the need to deal with each case on its merits using common sense and compassion, not cold, crude box-ticking methods or stringent, inflexible rules.

Such people shouldn't be threatened with losing benefits if they fail to find work they're neither comfortable with nor capable of doing. That's cruel and may be fatal.

And they should never, ever be made to feel bad about claiming – whether they run marathons or not. I hope that clears up any misunderstanding that might have arisen.

Turning to international news, more than 2,000 people have died in a massive earthquake in Nepal. Dozens of Brits are among the missing in the humanitarian crisis that's ensued.

This is terrible. It kinda puts things into perspective and makes you count your blessings, don't it?

April 28 – Bournemouth is party central at the moment. Why? – because our local football team has won promotion to the Premier League after a resounding 3–0 home win over Bolton yesterday evening.

It will be the first time the club's ever played in the top flight – but just six years ago it was a very different story.

Before I go into that, I must point out that technically speaking we're not quite there yet. The last games in the Championship, the second flight league AFC Bournemouth are in at the moment, are on Saturday.

But the way things stand, unless Middlesbrough beat Brighton by a 20-goal margin or Bournemouth lose away at Charlton by a similar score, it's in the bag thanks to our lads hitting the back of the net 95 times this season.

Watford have already secured their place in the Premier League, but if Sheffield Wednesday beat them Saturday and Bournemouth beat Charlton, our lads could go up as champions and Watford runners-up (The top two winning automatic promotion).

Middlesbrough would then have to fight it out in the play-off for the coveted third Premier League place.

It's hard to believe that just a few years ago the collection buckets were out and public meetings were being held in a desperate bid to save AFC Bournemouth – the Cherries – as the club faced extinction amid crippling debts.

Local people rallied round to help bail it out as it only just escaped being put into administration. And a last-day win in 2009 prevented it dropping out of the Football League altogether after a 17-point penalty had been imposed for its money troubles.

But since then its fortunes have improved no end thanks to Eddie Howe – former Cherries player, now manager – major investor Russian millionaire businessman Maxim Demin and some brilliant football taking the club steadily up the leagues.

This promotion takes the Cherries into the top flight for the first time in their history.

Although the exact date of the club's foundation is not known, there is proof that it was formed in the autumn of 1899 out of the remains of the older Boscombe St. John's Lads' Institute FC.

The club was originally known as Boscombe FC and some local people still call it that, as in the much-used phrase "back of the net Boscombe."

Back of the net indeed. Premier League here we come!

In other news, it's now known that more than 4,000 people were killed, 8,000 injured and about eight million affected by the earthquake in Nepal. Blimey!

And family entertainer Keith Harris has died at the age of 67 from cancer. The popular ventriloquist is best known for his cute nappy-wearing big green duck Orville, but I always preferred Cuddles, his naughty ginger monkey. I saw him with both of them once in a summer show at Bournemouth while on a family holiday from Slough.

April 30 – Had a lovely afternoon yesterday. As it was Bailey's third birthday, proud parents Sam and Carl held a little party at their home, attended by family members, friends and their children.

Resident mutt Albert, Bec's dog, had canine company in the form of her dad Russell's two Staffie bitches Blaze and Millie. And a good time was had by all, notably Bailey.

One of his presents was a mini drum kit which the kids had great fun banging as loudly as they could.

We all love Albert, a cute little brown Shih Tzu-terrier cross who reminds us all of Kelloggs, Sam's former ginger coloured doggie companion sadly no longer with us.

And jet-black Blaze has such a placid, sweet nature, just like Russell's former pet dog Lola, another Staffie but also now regretfully gone to the great kennel in the sky.

Millie, Blaze's young daughter, is a typically playful black and white puppy, even though she's bigger than her mum now.

Anyway, the dogs, the children and the adults all had a fine time. Sweet!

May 2 – Yesterday was a good one and a great way of kicking off the Mayday Bank Holiday weekend.

First off, I received a surprise visit from Phil, Emily and Chloe. We had coffee and a catch-up at my place and then went to the Commodore Hotel for lunch, returning to mine for a second cup of coffee before they left to go back home to Ferndown.

It was lovely seeing them again and nice to sit and chomp through a plate of bangers and mash while looking at the sea through the cliff top hotel's window.

Shortly after they left, I strolled up the road for a few birthday drinks with Sam, Carl and Becca, Sam's daughter, who was 19 yesterday. Bec's dad Russell, Jem Hannen, Sam's cousin Laura and Bec's friends Jade Millen and Joedie Watt were also there.

Early evening I went over to the Bell with Bec, Joedie and Ryan Millen, Jade's brother, for a couple more birthday drinks. While there I saw and chatted to my mates John Gaynor, Mark Hemington, Ben Avill and Lee Robertson.

Like I said, it was a good day all round and a mighty fine way of starting the bank holiday weekend.

But there was a tinge of sadness as we learned that R&B and soul singer Ben E King had died at the age of 76.

He started off making hits with the Drifters in the 1950s then went solo. He's probably best known for his sixties classic Stand By Me, in my opinion one of the coolest and greatest records to ever reach number one.

I've got the TV news on in the background and it's just been announced that the Duchess of Cambridge has given birth to a baby girl.

The new Royal baby will be fourth in line to the throne behind her granddad Prince Charles, her dad Prince William and her older brother Prince George, Kate and William's first-born who came into the world just under two years ago.

No doubt there will be celebrations all over the country and in many other parts of the world too.

May 3 – Whoop whoop! – AFC Bournemouth, the Cherries, are champions!

Having already made history by clinching promotion to the Premier League for the first time ever, they helped ensure they went up in style with a 3–0 away at Charlton in the last game of the Championship's season.

It had looked like they were going to finish second until Sheffield Wednesday scored a dramatic stoppage time equaliser against

Watford, robbing their hosts of victory and gifting the title to the Cherries by one point.

But even if the two top teams had ended up tied points-wise, Bournemouth would still have won thanks to a far better goal difference – 53 to Watford's 41.

The Cherries banged in 98 goals altogether this season – an amazing total. Brilliant!

What with seeing the family and helping Bec celebrate her birthday on Friday; it's turned into a pretty happy Bank Holiday weekend all round I'd say.

My friends Rebecca Browning and Nathan Trollope also had birthdays Friday.

And apart from toasting our local football team, Bournemouth folk are also joining the nation in having a few drinks in honour of the new Royal birth.

Not only that, I learnt on Facebook this morning that it's my friends Paul and Sarah's 17th anniversary of the day they got together. Many congrats guys!

The couple were fellow regulars at the Bell until moving to Wexford, Ireland, a few years back. They, too, support the Cherries and Manchester United.

Plus it's my cousin Sandra's birthday today – yet another reason to party.

But before we all get too carried away, please spare a thought for the poor people of Nepal, where the death toll has now risen to more than 7,000. I've lit a candle.

May 5 – Yesterday proved a fitting end to a wonderful Bank Holiday weekend for yours truly after all the aforementioned fun and celebration.

It was great to don my Cherries shirt and stroll in the sunshine to Boscombe Pier to see the start of Eddie and the lads' open top bus tour with the Championship trophy.

Apparently around 60,000 people packed the beach and prom between there and Bournemouth Pier as the manager and team were driven past.

I managed to get a vantage point in a car park overlooking Boscombe Pier – and from there I had a better view, albeit from a distance, than many people who had got closer as the players took it in turns to raise the gleaming cup to loud cheers and chants.

The atmosphere was electric and joyous and yes, I had a little tear in my eye.

Okay, I admit I don't attend football matches. I've never hidden the fact that I'm very much an armchair fan. I'll always follow the fortunes of Slough Town, my real home team, but I've lived in Bournemouth a lot longer now – 13 years longer in fact.

I've been a Manchester United fan since seeing George Best play on the telly in the mid-sixties and I've supported England since becoming interested in football as a boy.

But the Cherries are my adopted home side and their ground is in Kings Park, just up the road from here. I've watched their amazing and at times harrowing story unfold over the years with great anxiety and interest.

I was rooting for them as they escaped liquidation, extinction and going out of the Football League altogether – all by the skin of their teeth.

In January 1997, the club was so penniless a bucket collection was arranged at the Winter Gardens theatre in the town centre.

It was five minutes from liquidation just seven years ago and a year later the team was on the point of exiting the Football League when a precious Steve Fletcher goal ten minutes from time secured a crucial 2–1 win over Grimsby that saved the day.

Now we have the mouth-watering prospect of AFC Bournemouth playing in the same league as Liverpool, Arsenal, Chelsea, Tottenham, Everton, West Ham and the two Manchester giants next season.

It's a real life Roy of the Rovers story – only more incredible!

And when AFC Bournemouth competes directly with United? – Do you really need to ask? Much as I love Man U, at those times I'll be a proud Cherries fan – no question!

May 6 – Well, the new Royal baby's called Charlotte, or to give her full moniker Her Royal Highness Princess Charlotte Elizabeth Diana of Cambridge.

She's been named after her grandfather (Prince Charles), great-grandmother (Queen Elizabeth II) and grandmother (the late Princess Diana).

In other news, a second boat carrying migrants has sunk in the Med. Dozens of people drowned when an inflatable craft carrying an estimated 137 people went down south of Sicily. Terrible!

Oh and tomorrow's Election Day. Watch this space!

May 7 – It's just gone noon and earlier today I popped along to the polling station to cast my vote for the Greens in the general and local council elections.

Some will say this is a wasted vote as in Bournemouth it's realistically a two-party fight between the Tories and the Lib Dems with not even Labour standing a chance.

But this is defeatist talk, just like the whole idea of so-called tactical voting – that is, not choosing the person you really want but one of the others you don't want because they have a better chance of beating the candidate you definitely don't want to win.

This is nuts in my view and just props up a deeply flawed status quo mess that's the handiwork and tragic legacy of the three main parties.

There's no chance of ever having anything better unless people have the courage of their convictions and back the person and party they believe has the right ideas and will do the best job.

For me, that's the Greens – especially after Clegg and the Lib Dems so disgracefully betrayed me and other former long-time supporters.

I would never, ever vote Conservative because I despise with a passion most of what they stand for. The same applies to UKIP, the new right-wing kids on the block.

Seems to me Farage's party is a magnet for those who want a return to the bad old sexist, racist, homophobic days of the fifties and early sixties.

I share the frustration of those fed up to the back teeth with the big three's broken promises and I fully understand their wish to try something new. I'd just rather they picked Green, or the SNP in Scotland or Plaid Cymru in Wales, than UKIP.

There's been a lot of emotive alarmist bull crap spoken in the election build-up about people wanting to rip apart the United Kingdom – just like there was during the Scottish independence referendum last September.

Even if all the wild allegations were true, I say if that's what the majority of inhabitants in those regions want, why not give it them? I'm all for passing power back to the people at a more localised level.

That's one reason I'm a Green Party member now. We believe passionately in grass-roots democracy.

Okay, fair enough, I'm more armchair than activist. I don't do placards or meetings. But I've given cash, I spread the word in print and, unlike many, I do bother to vote.

It irritates me when people bang on about useless and corrupt politicians but do sod all about it – not even exercise their democratic right and duty in the simple task of putting a pencil cross on a piece of paper. I know some can't, but many more could.

A favourite excuse here is that politicians are all the same so what's the point? Now that really is being depressingly defeatist!

In truth the only wasted votes are the millions lost because people can't be arsed to use them. That's a disgrace.

Apart from the general election, another item on the news concerns the death of a famous singer.

The pop music world has been rocked to learn that Hot Chocolate lead vocalist Errol Brown has passed away at his Barbados home aged 71. He had liver cancer.

Errol and his group remain one of the smoothest, coolest acts ever to grace the pop charts and it was hard not to at least like them.

They had hits in more than 50 countries across the globe, including You Sexy Thing – which Brown co-wrote – It Started with a Kiss, Every 1's a Winner and the UK number one So You Win Again.

You Sexy Thing, number two in the mid-seventies, charted again in the eighties and also in 1997, when it reached number six after being used in the film *The Full Monty*.

Brown was made an MBE by the Queen in 2003 and received an Ivor Novello award for his outstanding contribution to British music in 2004.

No doubt radio stations will be playing lots of Hot Chocolate in the coming days and a best of compilation will top the charts very soon. Nothing wrong with that – nothing at all. RIP Errol, and thanks for the music.

May 8 – Happy birthday David, my brother-in-law, and Linda, a friend I made in Pokesdown who now lives back in her native Corsica.

I switched on the TV news this morning to learn some terrible news – we face another five years of Tory cuts and misery.

Yep, the Conservatives have won an overall majority in the general election. Bloody hell! It begs the obvious question – who the flipping heck voted for them?

With almost all seats declared, they have 325 MPs in the Commons against Labour's 229, enough to rule without the need for deals or coalitions.

Labour had a bad night and the Lib Dems a disastrous one – so much so that Nick Clegg has resigned as leader, though he was one of only eight of the party's MPs to keep their seats. They clinched 57 at the 2010 election.

But the real success story was the sensational achievement of the SNP in winning 56 of 59 Scottish seats, obliterating Labour north of the border.

Labour's leader Ed Miliband also quit in light of his party's unexpectedly poor result. All the pre-election opinion polls had shown them doing a lot better, keeping neck-and-neck with the Tories. Another hung Parliament had seemed inevitable.

The Commons' sole Green MP, Caroline Lucas, kept her Brighton seat by an increased margin as the party enjoyed its best election ever picking up nearly a million votes.

Sadly, the Greens could not gain any more seats thanks to our daft first past the post election system that also meant UKIP got three million votes but look like ending up with just one of the two MPs it started off with.

Nigel Farage has resigned as leader of UKIP having failed to gain the seat of South Thanet, losing out to Conservative candidate Craig Mackinlay.

Much as though I hate his party and its dreadful right-wing agenda, I and other Greens would totally sympathize with its supporters' frustration because we're suffering the same injustice. Why not allot seats in line with the nationwide totals of votes cast?

I've been a firm believer in proportional representation for some time now. Critics claim it's a recipe for uncertainty, indecision and hung Parliaments. I say look what happened last time around – and very nearly did again.

Farage wasn't the only high-profile loser last night. Labour's shadow chancellor Ed Balls and Lib Dems Vince Cable, former business secretary and Danny Alexander, former chief secretary to the treasury in the coalition government, were also ousted.

So was former Labour firebrand George Galloway, now leader of the Respect Party.

So we have Cameron and crew back in charge for another five years. Ye gods! But unlike last time, they do now have a clear mandate to rule under current election rules.

I'm absolutely staggered by this result. People had a golden opportunity to rid us of these despicable rulers who've spent five years inflicting pain and hardship on our poor nation. Why oh why didn't they take it?

I thought that the millions suffering job losses, firm closures, financial ruin, withdrawal of benefits or imposed poverty under these cruel, complacent and uncaring rich kids might have been eager to kick them out. Apparently not.

Was it a case of tactical voting, confused loyalties, apathy, an insane belief that they've done a good job, a deep dread of Labour or people thinking better the devil you know?

Search me. But there we have it.

I think a key turning point came in that televised live debate when Ed Miliband stubbornly refused SNP leader Nicola Sturgeon's offer of help to oust the Tories.

Obviously he wanted to win outright. But he instantly ruled out the prospect of a Labour-led government with support from other parties.

I feel that rash decision was a huge error of judgement that cost him dearly in lost votes – many of them going to his would-be allies in the Scottish polling booths.

It would have had the double-whammy effect of persuading some undecided voters to pick the Conservatives as the party possibly more likely to get a clear majority.

As a voter, I reserve the right to criticize the harsh, unjust right-wing measures we all know are on the way. But I now have to grudgingly accept that this is apparently the nation's majority will according to a system I want to be more properly democratic.

Cameron has pretty much got his own way without much opposition for the past half-decade. Now he's going to be insufferable and unstoppable as he continues his mad crusade to axe more real jobs and people's lifeline funds, hitting the poorest hardest.

I say real jobs as I hate the liberties being taken over zero hours contracts. I accept that some employers find the flexibility they offer invaluable in surviving financially. I also appreciate that such contracts might actually suit certain workers just fine.

That's why I didn't support Labour's plan to outlaw these contracts completely.

But I deeply resent the way they're cynically used to bump up the monthly employment figures while denying people access to state benefits if they decline the offer of such notoriously unpredictable work patterns with no financial guarantees.

To state the obvious, we all need reliable, regular incomes in order to pay our bills. Yet some callous employers, job centre staff, politicians and government officials choose to ignore this fact of life – with dire consequences for workers and claimants.

So, to sum up, smug, uncaring Cameron's back at Number 10. Good grief!

****

CHAPTER NINE – THE AFTERMATH

May 9 – Sam and Carl invited me to theirs yesterday for a few drinkies. It was nice to see her son Alex and his girlfriend Charley for a short while before they left to return to Wiltshire where they live and he's a chef.

Rudy and Bailey played in their room until bedtime and Becca was also there with her mate Joedie before they went out for the evening. Our friends Jem and Jimmy turned up later and Albert, Bec's little dog, sat on my lap quite a bit.

While searching on her laptop computer for background music to play, Sam located a track we hadn't heard for a while by the American rock band Matchbox 20. They really are superb, with great music and excellent poignant, profound, intelligent lyrics.

If you haven't heard anything of theirs, I'd recommend you check them out.

On a more serious note, we now have to face the aftermath of the general election. I think a lot of people are in for a really tough time.

May 10 – Another birthday, this time my friend Dean Toms – Deano – who I've had quite a few drinks with at the Bell over the years.

This weekend has seen various events across the country and continent marking the 70th anniversary of VE Day – May 8, 1945, when the war in Europe ended to joyous celebrations.

I was watching an old episode of the classic TV comedy series Only Fools and Horses the other day and one of those random memories popped into my head.

Wheeler-dealer Del Boy is ribbing younger brother Rodney over the fact he's never had a proper job but instead spent his working days acting as gofer for the family market trade business.

Del quips that Rodney's so well known at the local jobcentre that he gets invited to its staff parties.

This is a funny joke anyway but for me it carried a humorous ring of truth. A few years ago when I was on the dole, I was friends with a guy called Dave who worked at Boscombe Job Centre and used to drink in the Bell.

Dave rented a room at our mutual mate Paul Dangerfield's house in Roberts Road, Pokesdown – next door to where Sam and Carl now live.

I used to go round there to drink tinnies, smoke, chat, chill and listen to rock music in his room with him – such as Hawkwind singer Robert Calvert's brilliant solo albums.

Paul was often away long-distance lorry driving but his lady Sarah Basham was normally in the house, usually having a chat and laugh with a female friend.

Sarah and Paul now live in Wexford, Ireland and I've no idea what happened to Dave – I've not seen him for yonks. But I do know he left the jobcentre and his dream was to be an author.

But while still employed there he did once invite me along as he and his workmates had a curry in a local restaurant one Friday evening.

It was a good do as it goes – a fun night actually, with the added bonus that I got on first-name terms with the staff while still attending the dole office looking for work.

May 11 – What a sad day for football and music. It's the 30th anniversary of the Bradford fire that killed 56 people at a home tie against Lincoln City. And it's the date on which reggae legend Bob Marley died in 1981 – a great loss to pop culture.

I'm off to do some shopping in a mo so I'll light a candle for Bob and the blaze victims on my return.

It's now transpired that the local polls reflected the national picture with the Tories similarly tightening their grip on power.

In Bournemouth East, the Parliamentary seat for my neighbourhood, American-born Conservative candidate Tobias Ellwood, MP for the past 10 years, almost doubled his majority as the Lib Dems were pushed from second to fourth place behind the Labour and UKIP representatives.

Ellwood got 22,060 votes, Labour's Peter Stokes 7,448, UKIP's David Hughes 7,401, John Nicholas of the Lib Dems 3,752 and the Greens' Alasdair Keddie 3,263 – a great result for the party. Independent David Ross attracted 903.

In the Bournemouth Council elections – also held last Thursday – the Conservatives almost swept the board, gaining seven more seats to give them 51 out of 54. UKIP clinched an historic first as 21-year-old Laurence Fear won in the Kinson South ward.

The other two traditional rival parties were totally wiped out with Labour losing all three of its councillors and the Lib Dems their sole representative.

Particularly encouraging for me was the steady rise of the Greens locally as well as nationally. We amassed more votes than ever and got our first councillor in Simon Bull, who narrowly won one of three seats in Winton East after a tense recount.

The make-up of the council now stands at 51 Conservatives, one UKIP, one independent and one Green.

May 12 – Just because I try to be nice, that doesn't mean I'm dim or gullible. If you screw me over I'll know it, note it and remember it. But I'll still forgive you, blow you kisses and wish you well.

Spread the love girls and boys – spread the joy!

It saddens me when I see people so wrapped up in the physical aspects of life that they've completely lost any sense of the spiritual.

Some are so obsessed with material things they even think these are the measures of success and the pathways to contentment.

Okay, granted, no-one wants to live in abject poverty and I would moan like crazy if I had to give up some of my cherished creature comforts. Tragically, millions don't have that choice.

But it both depresses and frustrates me to see friends chuck treats and material possessions at others, especially children, thinking that's the way to ensure everyone's happy and full of love for their peers. It's not.

All people, and youngsters in particular, need nurturing, support and others' time, energy, advice and encouragement if they're going to be well-adjusted citizens having respect for and living in harmony with those around them.

Costly toys, trinkets and treats are all well and good, but they're not the be-all and end-all. If you lack an appreciation of the finer things in life and the sterling qualities of humanity, affection, consideration, wisdom and tolerance, it's not going to work.

Adult or child, you'll end up an unfulfilled, miserable pain in the backside – fact!

Speaking for myself, I've had a sense of the spiritual since childhood, initially through my Methodist upbringing and then via my own explorations into alternative belief systems. But I remained troubled and confused for years.

When writing *A New Perspective* (*Sunshine and Ice Volume One, Part Two*), I had a whole new exciting, energizing, exhilarating outlook and was bathing in an exquisite atmosphere of divine wisdom. I was feeling great. Not smug or superior, just great.

Then I was viciously assaulted and my soul took its terrifying descent into darkness, as explained in the book of the same name (*Sunshine and Ice Volume Two, Part One*).

Black cynicism took hold and I lost all trace of a spiritual sensibility. I still held the same liberal and inclusive religious beliefs but they were in my head only and no longer in my heart.

This deeply unsettling state of affairs lingered through my life-threatening cardiac crises (*Volume Three, Part Two*) and lasted until really quite recently as bad news, negative vibes and deeply unnerving developments continued to rock my world.

But now, at long last, I feel I'm beginning to regain my sense of spirituality, optimism and hope, partly thanks to the encouraging and enlightening literature I'm reading.

I've just finished *Your Life After Death* and I've now started on *The Fall and Revelation*, two more books by medium and author Michael G Reccia.

As I've already mentioned, this guy claims to channel Joseph, an ancient and highly-evolved spiritual entity said to have made contact with the material world to impart divine wisdom as a matter of urgency in a bid to help avoid a looming apocalypse.

I know it sound more than a bit far-fetched and wildly alarmist, but actually it's not.

The books, published by Band of Light Media, are in a series called *The Joseph Communications*, and in fact their bottom line assertion is joyous and comforting.

Basically, Joseph is saying that each one of us is a spiritual entity, a soul, wrapped in a physical body – a tiny droplet of the infinite ocean of existence, the One God that is both our original source and the home we will all eventually return to.

We're all spiritual beings trying to live in badly flawed material world, and our Earth has twice faced cataclysms and had to start all over again. History's about to repeat itself unless we change direction fast. The good news is that it's within our power.

The even better news is that our souls will live on regardless.

But, like Joseph via Michael, I'm trying to use clumsy words to convey complex, subtle, highly-refined and exceedingly deep spiritual concepts.

A lot of what he says echoes the Bible story of the Garden of Eden, the vivid poetry of John Milton's *Paradise Lost* and the legend of Atlantis.

I retain my open, questioning mind at all times, and I must confess it all sounds outlandish in the extreme.

I fully understand and share people's natural scepticism and their fear that Michael's not exactly genuine so we're being fed a load of religious hogwash.

But there's an undeniable ring of authenticity and authority here – a far more intelligent, balanced, persuasive, all-encompassing and sophisticated form of divine wisdom than I've found in any other books or texts grappling with the metaphysical.

It does make me wonder where this amazing, enlightening, comforting and life-affirming information is coming from. Wherever it is, it all sounds good to me.

But it goes further than that. Thanks to these books, I'm starting to at last feel I'm on the way back to where I was before it all went pear shaped for me personally.

And I can't over-emphasize how flipping great that feels. The only problem is I now have to try and stay upbeat, spiritually-aware and positive – a tall order in our mundane reality infested by negative vibes and obsessively materially-minded people.

I'm just as vulnerable as the next person to succumb to persistent and corrosive mindsets that cause friction and division – aspects of the dark negative force that keeps us bound and chained in our deeply flawed physical existence.

I hate it when I get petty and bitchy, which happens far too often for my liking. It's a constant struggle, and it's much easier to give in and allow the mire to suck me down.

All this talk about divinity and highly evolved spiritual beings reminds me of that Illuminati website where the guy claiming to be their spokesman refers to humans as potentially divine beings needing to evolve into higher forms of themselves.

This certainly runs parallel to Joseph's assertions but there's a massive difference in emphasis. Joseph's words are full of hope and joy, light and love, whereas the Illuminati feller's vision is far darker, colder, more clinical and ultimately depressing.

For example, Joseph, through Michael, speaks of Atlantis – and so does the anonymous Illuminati guy. They refer to the same legend, but in vividly contrasting ways. Give me Joseph's version any time!

I guess that's the bottom line really – much of what the Illuminati says strikes a chord with me on but an intellectual level only as the overall message seems spiritually bankrupt. Joseph, on the other hand, fills my soul with joy.

I'm sure a lot of this depends on whether you're an artist or a scientist. I find it intriguing that very few people are good at both English and mathematics. Most are quite skilled in one but rubbish at the other.

English is my forte and I struggle with maths. Friends of mine are the other way around. It reminds me of American author Robert Pirsig's classic book *Zen and the Art of Motorcycle Maintenance*.

He similarly divides people into romantics and classics. Romantics relish in abstracts, imagery, ideas, dreams and all forms of art, classics stick to cold hard facts and remain obsessively logical and analytical.

I'm the first without question. That's why I'd rather go with Joseph's bright and uplifting version of ultra-realities than the Illuminati's clinical, grey, soulless and rather brutal one.

The world needs physicists and mathematicians, but it also needs poets and musicians. The pragmatic and the imaginative need each other more than they often realize.

Hold on tight people, we're being returned to Earth with a juddering crash, thanks to that ridiculous man Nigel Farage.

He announced his resignation as UKIP leader on Friday, the day after he failed to win the South Thanet Parliamentary seat in the general election.

But any hopes that we might have seen the back of him have been dashed by the news he's un-resigned himself.

The official story is that he tendered his resignation but UKIP chiefs refused to accept it and invited him to stay on, and on reconsidering his position, he has. What a farce!

This crazy media-attracting circus just about sums up Farage and his ludicrous limelight-hogging right-wing band of eccentric nut jobs and allegedly sexist, homophobic foreigner-haters apparently stuck in a 1950's time warp.

What's really rich is the fact that they accused comedian Al Murray of making a mockery of the election campaign when in fact they were similarly doing so.

Murray, in his character of the hilariously xenophobic Pub Landlord, stood himself in South Thanet, attracting 318 votes. The Tory candidate won and UKIP was second, Labour third, the Green Party next and the Lib Dem guy fifth.

But UKIP did win control of Thanet Council, its first district authority in the UK. And it did pick up three million votes across the nation and kept one of its two Commons seats. So Farage and co have plenty to smile about as they continue their mad crusade.

Al Murray was indeed mocking the election in general and UKIP in particular. But I say UKIP members themselves are taking the mick with their deliberately absurd and confrontational comments and manifesto.

Keeping with the mundane, a new series of Benefits Street started last night on Channel Four, with the setting switching from a council estate in Birmingham to one in Stockton-on-Tees. It's equally absorbing and controversial.

Just like series one, it shows financially-strapped residents resorting to crime to keep afloat financially as their benefits are cut and any hopes of work disappear over the horizon. This is Cameron's Britain – I hope he's very proud of it. Because I'm not.

I'm ashamed at the mess the politicians have left our country in and the desperate plight of many of its citizens. This is not only Cameron, Osborne and Clegg's legacy, it's Brown and Blair's too, and our beleaguered nation's political leaders before them.

While our Tory Prime Minister pats himself on the back and outrageously claims we're emerging from the woods thanks to him, the residents of council estates in Stockton, Birmingham and elsewhere bear testimony to consistent political failure.

This is broken Britain indeed – a shattered nation beset with problems thanks to our smug, uncaring and cruel Parliamentary overlords with their insane policies. Nice!

See what I mean about getting embroiled in negative vibes and sucked into the mire? I try so hard to stay chirpy, spiritually focussed and positive, but the dirty, heavy, dark and draining mud of physical existence continually drags me down. Sad but true.

But there are shafts of light, some of them provided in programmes like this. One thing that struck me about the Stockton folk was that, just like the Brummies in series one, they had a real community spirit sadly lacking in many more affluent areas.

May 13 – Dozens of people have died in a second major earthquake in Nepal. Rescue and aid teams from all over the world are continuing their efforts to help survivors.

May 14 – My granddaughter Chloe is two today. Happy birthday, precious girl – see you at your party in Ferndown on Saturday. I also extend birthday greetings to my good pal Theresa Bevis and also Leesa, my close friend Carole Jones's daughter.

Theresa is 50, so is just entering her golden years, just like several of my other mates have done recently. I wish them all well.

I've been playing some Motorhead CDs over the past couple of days or so. Lemmy has written some great songs, he's one fine lyricist and the words to the outstanding track Orgasmatron are especially brilliant.

I've also recently been listening to a couple of Galahad albums, a bit of Don McLean, Lindisfarne, Sinead O'Connor, the Las, Matchbox 20 and AC/DC.

And I'm currently playing Their Greatest Hits by Hot Chocolate as a tribute to Errol Brown. Oh I do love to mix it up a bit!

On the DVD front, I've been enjoying watching the Inbetweeners series one and two and the first series of the wonderfully surreal comedy show The Mighty Boosh.

On telly, it's been the soaps, Benefits Street, a similar programme entitled Skint, Russell Howard's Good News, a gripping drama called the Safe House, satirical puppet show Newzoids, the new series of Inspector George Gently, the Paul O'Grady Show and re-runs of old episodes of Only Fools and Horses, Marple, New Tricks, Family Guy, Sherlock, Columbo and Midsomer Murders.

I like my soaps, crime dramas and comedy programmes – and some documentaries.

May 15 – Finishing of the week in a typically eclectic musical vein, I've been playing albums featuring Bob Marley and King Crimson.

I'm just about to hear the end of A Young Person's Guide to King Crimson, a superior "best of" collection if ever I heard one.

Songs like Starless, the Night Watch, Ladies of the Road, Epitaph, Moonchild, Cadence and Cascade, I Talk to the Wind, Cat Food, Book of Saturday, Red and the Court of the Crimson King are timeless classics. I love this CD!

Earlier I played the Wailers' excellent album Catch a Fire in tribute to the late, great Bob, who died 34 years ago this week. I mentioned this on the 11th, the anniversary.

We heard on this morning's news that another musical icon, blues pioneer and maestro B B King had died aged 89. He helped inspire many rock guitarists including George Harrison, Keith Richards, Jimmy Page and Richie Sambora (Bon Jovi) and laid down some really cool tracks with many artists including Eric Clapton and U2.

Flicking through the TV channels last night to find something to watch, I came across Ron Howard's film *Angels and Demons*, so I stuck with that and recorded it too on my Tivo box.

Just like *The Da Vinci Code*, which I have on DVD, it stars Tom Hanks as Professor Robert Langdon, an acknowledged expert in religious and occult symbolism through the ages.

Both are thrillers based on books written by Dan Brown, who ties together all manner of myths and legends to produce gripping yarns.

The Da Vinci Code centred on controversial allegations that Jesus survived crucifixion to father children with Mary Magdalene, establishing a closely-guarded and zealously-protected Royal bloodline that continues to this day.

Angels and Demons, a later film but based on the earlier of the two bestselling novels, features our old friends the Illuminati – here portrayed as very much the bad guys bent on destroying the Roman Catholic Church by exploding a bomb in Vatican City, killing thousands of innocent people in the process.

It's another fast-paced, race-against-time roller-coaster ride with a similar happy ending. And, just like *The Da Vinci Code*, it raises the kind of questions conspiracy addicts love to weave their outlandish theories around.

Readers of my published work will know that I find all this sort of stuff fascinating. But let's get one thing straight. These books and films are fiction, pure and simple.

The intriguing question, of course, is how much they are based on fact. Some will say they get pretty close to very uncomfortable truths, others will claim they're total fantasy. It must come as no surprise that I try to keep an open mind.

But I tend to veer closer to the conspiracy camp because I'm firmly convinced that, mixed in with all the myths, legends and modern-day story-telling are hard facts about the dark, self-obsessed elite that runs our world – whether it's the Illuminati or not.

I'm certain that the reality we're programmed to accept is only part of the picture and sinister individuals are at work behind the scenes while their lackeys help shield us from unpalatable aspects of the whole situation.

By the way, Illuminati means "illuminated ones" and the bloke on that website I've referred to claims they're the enlightened good guys wanting a better world for us all.

They do indeed hate the Roman Catholic Church and all forms of organised religion – Christian, Jewish, Islamic and the rest – which they say are savage instruments of control, oppression and exploitation from which they want to set us free.

And these intellectual men of science, maths and logic wish to persuade us that blind faith is holding us back and theirs is the only way forward, the means to bring out our own inner divine nature and take ourselves to the next level of spiritual evolution.

But, as I've said, I find their vision rather joyless, soulless and ultimately brutal. It seems to lack heart. The emphasis on cold rationality and hard maths is too clinical.

Oh, and all the talk of angels and demons are vivid religious picture language rather than anything put forward by these avid advocates of harsh reason.

I think we're all part angel, part demon as our inner positive and negative energy currents constantly battle to control our minds, therefore our words and actions.

I'd rather live in a world of magic and miracles than maths and the mundane.

I fully accept that numbers can be magical, there is such a thing as sacred geometry, we couldn't have music or poetry without some appreciation of form and structure, and figures in their diverse manifestations are the bedrock of our conventional reality.

I think it's so sad when fixed formulas, cold calculations and stony statistics become king and people lose all perception of beauty, mystery, warmth and imagination.

Yep, I'm an artist, a romantic, and an optimist – albeit with a cynical streak – where others are scientists, classics and pessimists. My glass is half-full, not half-empty. I'm more passionate than pragmatic. I love English and struggle with mathematics.

That's how it is – and I wouldn't have it any other way. But at the same time I must accept that I'm a bit of a puzzling paradox.

I'm organised, very methodical and I love routine. I like to plan ahead and know what's going on from one minute to the next. I don't usually do spontaneous and indecision, uncertainty, chopping, changing and surprises can do my head in.

So in those respects I guess I'm a lot more fixed than flexible, disciplined than daring, pragmatic than poetic, classic than creative.

But that's my head taking control of my own circumstances. In the wider world, and following my deepest instincts, I'm very much with the artists and dreamers.

Religions are saturated with colourful but misleading and far too simplistic imagery.

For example, referring to God as our father is an attempt to convey a complicated relationship in language people will understand. You could just as easily speak of God as our mother – but Y'shua (Jesus) was speaking to people in a very patriarchal society where women were very much regarded as second-class citizens.

So the idea behind the father description was to make that blatantly biased community understand the nature of God as a loving, nurturing, guiding parent.

In fact, God is way beyond narrow gender definitions and we are all aspects of this original source of everything – humans, animals, plants, landscapes, the Earth itself, the sun, moon, universe and galaxies.

We each have a spark of divinity – God – within us and we're all destined to return home to that all-embracing Oneness. Our spirits or souls are all single expressions of God but most have forgotten or choose to rubbish or ignore this vital fact of life.

This is very deep and profound stuff and I was as gobsmacked as anyone else when David Icke declared he was the son of God on telly to angry cries of "blasphemy!"

But Christianity teaches that we're all God's children and the Lord's Prayer even starts with the word "Our Father, who art in Heaven…"

Trouble is, somewhere along the way something went badly wrong and we became bogged down in this seriously limited, imperfect deeply unsatisfactory physical existence with all its negative muck, friction, problems, pain and ideas of separation.

This ancient occurrence is variously portrayed in the stories of the Garden of Eden, the legend of Atlantis and John Milton's concept of Satan as a fallen angel in his epic poem *Paradise Lost*.

But again, the truth is far subtler than all this rather striking but crude imagery.

I'm convinced that some of the negatively-influenced manipulators of reality, people and events are as knowledgeable of these complex ultra-realities and skilled in employing them as those working to promote the forces of love and light.

This is precisely why the sinister elite pulling strings from the shadows are so dangerous – they know how to twist reality as we know it to their own ends.

And it's obvious from that Illuminati website that whoever's behind it is just as well-versed in such metaphysical matters and the idea that we are each potentially divine.

But they see science as our saviour, not religion.

The way I see it, there needn't be conflict between the two, which are both fields of expression of God that have become perceived as contradictory, suiting some unscrupulous puppet masters on both sides of the false divide very well indeed.

In fact, science and religion are both fragmented aspects of Oneness but they've been cynically and deliberately set up as rivals by trusted people bent on controlling minds.

So, if you like, the Biblical creation story and the Big Bang Theory are each an expression or aspect of the whole truth of how our universe and others came about.

I've thought such things for a while now – and people like David Icke have definitely helped put me on what I consider the right track – but Michael G Reccia's books tie all these ideas and concepts together in the most joyous, intelligent and complete way.

Whether or not you believe an ancient and wise spiritual entity can speak through a modern-day medium, there's undeniable wisdom here, no matter what the source.

I'd thoroughly recommend these publications to open-minded truth seekers

May 16, evening – Tomorrow will be tinged with sadness – it would have been Jan's birthday – but today's been very pleasant indeed. It was Chloe's party in Ferndown, attended by family and friends.

It's always great to see Phil, Emily and my grandchildren and it was nice to catch up again with Em's parents Gail and Keith, her sister Rachel with baby Lily, brother Simon, Joe, Cheryl, her daughter Kayleigh and other members of my extended family.

But I have other reasons to smile.

Next month sees the second anniversary of the publication of my first book, *Sunshine and Ice Volume One*. Volumes two to nine are also out there and this one, volume 10, is nearing completion and will be winging its way to my publishers within days.

I'm chuffed to bits that at long last I feel I'm regaining my sense of the spiritual. I'll continue to read books that inspire me in this.

So on these happy notes, I wish to begin wrapping up this latest instalment of my life story, lyric collection and assorted comments and ramblings.

But I'm far from complacent and I'm acutely aware that I'm just as liable to slip back into negative thought patterns and petty bitching as the next person. That's why I try to empathize rather than criticize.

Whether or not I end up completing any more books for publication, I shall persevere with my quest to entertain, inform and maybe even help point others towards enlightenment with my nutty views and comments. Now that would be cool!

I hope I'm doing a good PR job for green politics, spiritual thinking, common sense, humour and plain old fashioned decency. My ultimate goal is to help strengthen the positive vibration and assist in the dispersal of that deeply destructive negative one.

I'll continue to recommend TV programmes, movies, books, music and websites that I feel touch on aspects of the truth in an intelligent, illuminating or light-hearted way.

My time will be spent writing, reading, socialising with friends, seeing family, watching telly, listening to music, plucking away at my acoustic bass and six-string guitars, walking to the cliff top to sit overlooking the sea, doing my light exercises, cooking, eating, sleeping, shopping and cleaning my flat.

Apart from pub sessions, the very occasional gig, local community events and possibly very short breaks not too far away, that's about it. And that suits me fine.

I no longer have the energy for a more hectic existence, and besides, too much activity and excitement could be hazardous to my health.

All in all, I'm enjoying my life in Bournemouth with its lovely views and recently promoted football team.

But I remember my roots in Slough and I also vividly remember all the times of tragedy, trauma, tribulations and tears I've encountered to get to this point.

Keep the faith, keep smiling and keep those glittering stars shining brightly, lighting the way to a better future for us all.

Spread the love, sisters and brothers

Peace

> *The spark of consciousness in this body called*
> *Martin Money, May 16, 2015*

****

"When the power of love overcomes the love of power, the world will know peace"– Jimi Hendrix, 27/11/1942 to 18/9/1970.

"The revolution is just a tee-shirt away" – Billy Bragg, 1988

Let's get a little love in here
Get a little love in here
We all need it – now ain't that clear? –
So let's get a little love in here – Martin Money, 1976 and 2012

With lyrics so colourful, music so sweet
Those rock and roll poets make my life complete
— Martin Money, 2015

I'd rather live in a world of magic and miracles than maths and mediocrity.

Just because I try to be nice, that doesn't mean I'm dim or gullible. If you screw me over I'll know it, note it and remember it. But I'll still forgive you, blow you kisses and wish you well.

Spread the love girls and boys – spread the joy!

Our individual pasts can't be changed but we should work together to improve our shared future – for all our sakes.

****

This book is written as a loving tribute to Mum, Dad, Jan, John, Auntie Sylvia and my Uncles Bert, Jack and Fred – all sadly passed over.

In fond memory of Yvonne & Den Collins, Tom & Ruth Dixon, Gladys Weston, Bill Dutfield, Umo, Hairy Pete, Mike Hannen, Samantha, Tarrant, Canadian Mike, Lee.

Furthermore, it is dedicated with immeasurable love to Phil, Emily, Chloe, Lucas, Harvey, Carol & David, Auntie Joyce, Suzette, Sandra & Alan and my wider family.

Love and thanks also to Joe, Dawn, Paula, Carole, Shaz, Tom, Chris & family, Linda, Cheryl, Kerry, Theresa, Claire, Steve Y, Jill, Torben, Steve M, John C, the Dominoes.

Sam, Carl, Rudy, Bailey, Becca, Alex, Charley, Diane, Jac, Laura, Russell, Jimmy, Sonia, Sharon, Cass, Jade, Ryan, Joedie, Lillie and the other Roberts Road randoms.

Jem, Bridget,& Co, Johns G & P, Billy, Big Sam, Tina W, Steve E, Paul & Sarah, Jobcentre Dave, Roz, Tina & Jeff, Chris & Lou, Rod, Andy, Rich, Darren & Tara.

Brun, Lisa, Lawrence, the two Kellys, Trudy, Lou & family, DJ Steve, Paul S, Craig, Emily, Vicky & Mark, Tim, Diana S, Rob the Leg, Squaddie Nick, Dan S, Debs & Al.

Jen C, Maria S, Quiz Paul, Bev, Mich, Bill, Maria H, Jane M, Dottie, Dean, Paul M.

Laura, Mark, Sam, Dave, Beccy & Gary, Matt & Dani, Ben, Jenny, Tich, Clare, Jim, Ollie, Stu & Melody, Lee, Darren S, Ross, Dawn, Penny, Gemma and other Bell faces.

Steve G, Andy, Jerry, Diane & Chris, Peter P, Connie & Ski, Terry, Kevin, and others from those golden Pinecliff, Home Guard, White Horse, Portman & Palmerston days.

Super local bands we saw such as the Blue Cadillacs, Hippo, Ricky and the Cufflinks the Flaming Softies, Rocky and the Hurricanes and Frank Slob & the Slobettes.

Milk Marketing Martin and school pals Dave T, Steve B, Terry S, Chris T, Chris Z.

Lorna, Sue, June, Noreen, Patsy, Wendy, Sylvia, Faron and the Krypton/Mace crew.

And everyone else mentioned in Chapter Nine, Volume Seven, Persistent Illusions.

If I've forgotten you I apologize – I salute every single person who's enriched my life in any way, whether still physically with us or passed on. Cheers for everything guys!

ABOUT THE AUTHOR

Born in Slough on February 25, 1954, Martin Money lived there until early adulthood, moving to Dorset in 1978.

Leaving school with three A Levels and seven O Levels, he worked in a bank for a few months before starting a 24-year career in regional journalism that ended in redundancy in 1997.

Since then he's had a variety of part-time jobs and also worked as a volunteer for charities.

A proud father and grandfather, he lives in Bournemouth where he enjoys short cliff-top walks, writing, reading, watching TV, listening to music and socialising.

Author's photo by Sam Excell

www.ingramcontent.com/pod-product-compliance
Lightning Source LLC
Chambersburg PA
CBHW031227250726
48655CB00005B/1834